Getting StartED with Mac OS X Leopard

Justin Williams

friendsof

DESIGNER TO DESIGNER™

an Apress company*

Getting StartED with Mac OS X Leopard

Credits

Lead Editor
Jeffrey Pepper

Technical Reviewer
Carlos Castillo

Editorial Board
Steve Anglin, Ewan Buckingham,
Tony Campbell, Gary Cornell,
Jonathan Gennick, Jason Gilmore,
Kevin Goff, Jonathan Hassell,
Matthew Moodie, Joseph Ottinger,
Jeffrey Pepper, Ben Renow-Clarke,
Dominic Shakeshaft, Matt Wade, Tom Welsh

Senior Project Manager
Tracy Brown Collins

Senior Copy Editor
Ami Knox

Assistant Production Director
Kari Brooks-Copony

Production Editor
Laura Esterman

Compositor
Dina Quan

Artist
April Milne

Proofreader
April Eddy

Indexer
Tim Tate

Interior and Cover Designer
Kurt Krames

Manufacturing Director
Tom Debolski

CONTENTS AT A GLANCE

CONTENTS

CONTENTS

ABOUT THE AUTHOR

Justin Williams is the owner and lead developer of Second Gear, a web and software development firm located in Evansville, Indiana. He is a 2006 graduate of Purdue University with a degree in computer and information technology. Justin is the editor and lead writer for MacZealots (www.maczealots.com). He also writes a weekly technology column in the *Evansville Courier & Press.* His personal blog, carpeaqua, can be found at www.carpeaqua.com.

Justin spends his free time watching TV, playing video games, and working out.

ABOUT THE TECHNICAL REVIEWER

Carlos Castillo has more than 13 years of experience in training, repairs, and administration of Apple and PC computers. His love for the industry keeps him busy with his own IT consulting business, Mac mini carputer project, tech reviewing books, beta testing for Apple developers like Bruji and Twisted Melon, and database management. In 2004, Carlos did a 13-month tour in Iraq (OIF2) and is now a staff sergeant in the California Army National Guard. Carlos lives in West Los Angeles, California, with his wife, Rosie. When not working or deployed, he enjoys traveling, photography, and spending time with his family.

1 MAC OS X LEOPARD'S NEW FEATURES

Every 12 to 24 months, Apple changes the world when it releases the latest version of its operating system, Mac OS X (pronounced "Mac OS Ten"). Mac OS X is the successor to the classic Mac OS that was originally released in 1984 along with the original Macintosh. Mac OS X was built off of the NeXT technology that Apple purchased in 1997. The classic Mac OS had begun to show its age in the late 1990s as Microsoft's Windows operating system enjoyed features such as multiuser support, multitasking, and memory protection. NeXT's NeXTStep OS gave Apple a starting point for building a next-generation OS that would last them another 10 years.

History of Mac OS X

Since its initial release in 2001, Mac OS X has seen five major releases, as illustrated in Figure 1-1, and with Leopard, Apple has introduced its sixth incarnation of OS X. First released in March 2001, Mac OS X 10.0 was codenamed Cheetah and was generally thought of as not ready for primetime. While the OS was stable, it was still missing important features like DVD playback and was incredibly slow on modern hardware. Apple realized this, and in September 2001 released Mac OS X 10.1 (codename Puma). Mac OS X 10.1 Puma was released as a free upgrade to anyone who had purchased the original version. Besides implementing DVD playback, Puma was much faster than its predecessor.

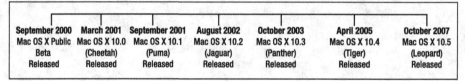

September 2000	March 2001	September 2001	August 2002	October 2003	April 2005	October 2007
Mac OS X Public	Mac OS X 10.0	Mac OS X 10.1	Mac OS X 10.2	Mac OS X 10.3	Mac OS X 10.4	Mac OS X 10.5
Beta	(Cheetah)	(Puma)	(Jaguar)	(Panther)	(Tiger)	(Leopard)
Released	Released	Released	Released	Released	Released	Released

Figure 1-1. A timeline of the history of Mac OS X releases

Each version of Mac OS X is attached with a codename through its development cycle. Up to this point, Apple has used large cats for these codenames. There are quite a few cats that Apple could still use, so I would infer that the naming scheme would continue well into the future.

About a year after the release of 10.1, Apple released version 10.2, codenamed Jaguar. Jaguar introduced Quartz Extreme, which improved the graphical performance of the operating system by outsourcing the drawing routines onto the graphics card rather than the CPU. Jaguar also introduced current staples in the Mac experience like the systemwide AddressBook framework, Rendezvous (now called Bonjour) network discovery, and iChat.

While most Mac users were pleased with the Jaguar release of Mac OS X, many touted Mac OS X 10.3 Panther as the release that cemented Mac OS X as ready for primetime. Panther introduced the brushed-metal Finder windows, audio and video chat in iChat, and the Safari web browser. Panther also added fast user switching to allow multiple users to be logged in to a single Mac at the same time and Exposé, which at the time was seen as a revolutionary way to deal with window clutter on your desktop.

Mac OS X Panther was the beginning of the slower pace of evolution in the Mac OS X platform. The first four releases all arrived in a 3-year time span. A lot of this change was done mostly to bring Mac OS X up to the same level as that of Mac OS 9 prior to its death. After Panther's release, Apple took its time perfecting the next release of the OS, Tiger, which was released in April 2005.

Mac OS X Tiger introduced the Spotlight search technology, which made finding content on your Mac easy. Spotlight changed the way we searched on our computers by allowing users to search not only by the file name, but also the contents **inside** a file.

Tiger's other major featured was the introduction of the Dashboard, shown in Figure 1-2. Dashboard allowed your Mac to run miniature applications called **widgets** that would be superimposed over your regular desktop. These widgets usually performed a single task such as getting the weather forecast, showing the time in another city or country, or translating a string of text from one language to another.

Figure 1-2. Mac OS X 10.4 Tiger's Dashboard

At Apple's Worldwide Developers Conference in June 2005, Apple released a version of Mac OS X Tiger that ran on Intel-based Macintoshes. Prior to that point, all Macs had been running on PowerPC-based chips built by IBM and Motorola. Apple released the final version of Mac OS X Tiger for Intel at Macworld in January of 2006. For all intents and purposes, the PowerPC and Intel version of Tiger are exactly the same, save for the chip architecture they are built to run on.

Now in 2007, Apple has released the successor to Mac OS X Tiger, codenamed Leopard.

What's new in Mac OS X Leopard

Mac OS X Leopard is seen as a release that will further extend Mac's lead against Windows in terms of innovation by improving the user experience for Mac users. Besides adding in many new features, Apple also focuses on refining applications that you already know and love like iChat and iCal. Following is a brief overview of some of the new features in Mac OS X Leopard.

A new desktop

If you have used a previous version of Mac OS X, you are bound to notice that on the surface there are some subtle changes to the user interface. Apple has updated the look of the desktop to include a semitransparent menu bar (the white bar at the top of your screen). The standard Mac OS X Dock has also received an updated look, with each icon lying on a reflective glass floor.

Apple has also taken the time to unify the Mac OS X interface so that each window has the same look and feel to it. No longer will one of your applications have a brushed-metal look similar to iTunes and the next have a standard Aqua feel like Mail. Each window features the same dark-gray look.

A new Finder

The Finder has seen its biggest change since Mac OS X Panther. Each Finder window's sidebar now has all your devices, shared machines, folders on your Mac, and saved searches logically grouped in a method similar to iTunes. Also borrowed from iTunes is Finder's new **Cover Flow view**, which lets you preview your files and folders by navigating through them like you would a group of albums. I will be covering the new Finder more in the next chapter.

Time Machine

The major feature of Leopard is the new backup system called **Time Machine**. Time Machine makes backing up your Mac as simple as plugging in an external hard drive and letting OS X handle the rest. No longer will you have to worry about losing your important documents, photos, and videos due to a computer crash because everything will be archived on a secondary drive. What's more, Time Machine can save multiple copies of each file as determined by the interval you set. You'll get a chance to learn more about Time Machine in Chapter 8.

Spaces

Mac OS X Leopard also includes a new feature called **Spaces** that brings multiple desktop support to your Mac. You can use Spaces to organize the windows you are working with in logical (or illogical) separate desktops, as shown in Figure 1-3. You could create a desktop for your Mail and iChat conversations, one for your web browsing, and one to edit your digital photos. Prior to Spaces, you would need multiple monitors to accomplish something like this: now you just need a Mac running Leopard. Chapter 7 covers Spaces, as well as Exposé.

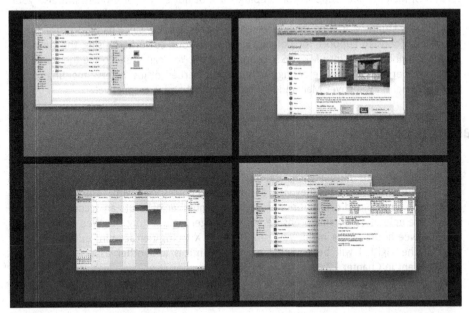

Figure 1-3. Mac OS X Leopard's Spaces feature makes it easy to organize multiple virtual desktops in any way you see fit—all on a single physical monitor.

Spotlight

Besides the new features, Leopard is focused on refining the existing Mac user experience to be even richer. Apple has added support for using Spotlight to search other Macs over your network. Spotlight in Leopard also adds a quick preview so that you can get an idea of what a document or photo contains from within the Spotlight window. I will be discussing Spotlight in depth in Chapter 3.

iChat

iChat also has seen many substantial changes. The biggest change is that iChat now supports tabbed chats, which consolidates all of your open iChat conversations into a single window. iChat also allows for multiple logins so that you can keep more than one AIM or Jabber account online simultaneously. There are also many AV changes to make video chats even more fun than before. I will be discussing iChat and Safari in depth in Chapter 5.

iCal and Mail

Leopard also has a focus on making personal information management easier. The new version of Mail includes support for keeping track of not only your e-mails, but also your to-do lists and short notes. Mail also supports stationery so that you can send e-mails that look visually stunning. iCal has also received its biggest update since its original release in Jaguar. iCal adds in support for collaborating with your coworkers using the new iCal Server technology built into Mac OS X Leopard Server. You can use it to see the schedules of your coworkers, schedule meetings with multiple parties, or just reserve meeting rooms and equipment. I will cover Mail and iCal in Chapters 4 and 9, respectively.

Parental controls

Mac OS X has had basic parental controls for a while, but with Leopard parental controls have gotten an extreme makeover. Parents can now restrict what applications their children can run, what web sites they visit, and who they correspond with. Leopard also introduces time limits based on the time of day or the number of hours an account is logged in. For example, if you want to ensure your teenager isn't surfing the Web and chatting into the wee hours of the night, you can force OS X to log her account out at a certain time of the night. I will be covering parental controls and other aspects of account management in Chapter 17.

Summary

Hopefully, this chapter whets your appetite for what is to come in later chapters as you discover Mac OS X Leopard. In the next chapter, I'll be giving you a full course in getting up and running on your Mac with Mac OS X Leopard. By the end of the chapter, you should have a solid foundation of knowledge to build upon throughout the rest of the book.

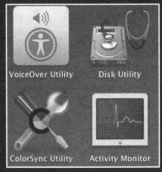

Before you can dive into all the neat features of Mac OS X Leopard, you need a basic foundation to build on. If you're coming from a Windows background, adjusting to some of the differences between Mac OS X and Windows can be daunting. Windows and Mac OS X follow several differing paradigms in terms of user interface design, user experience, and ease of use. It's not that either version is necessarily wrong—each is just different.

This chapter takes a look at the basic Mac OS X desktop and what each part entails. I'll introduce you to the basic interface elements such as the **menu bar**, **Dock**, and **Apple menu**. I'll also cover how the Mac organizes your files, folders, and applications. Finally, I'll introduce you to the **Finder**, the application used to work with your files.

By the end of the chapter, you should be comfortable with the basics of the Mac platform and working with your files and folders.

Ready? Let's get started!

The Mac desktop

When you first launch your Mac running Leopard, you will notice that there are four basic elements: the menu bar, the Dock, the desktop itself, and the desktop picture (see Figure 2-1).

Figure 2-1. The basic Mac OS X Leopard desktop

The menu bar

Along the top of the window is a semitransparent menu bar. The menu contains four distinct elements. To the far left is the Apple menu (looks like an apple). This menu is visible at all times and in all applications because it is where you click to do universal tasks such as restarting or shutting down your Mac.

Next to the Apple menu is the application menu, in bold, and any subsequent menus associated with the active application. The application menu shows the name of the application you are currently using (in this case Finder). The menu gives you access to the application's preferences and the ability to hide or quit the application. Subsequent menus are related to actions you can perform in that application.

To the far right, you will see several menu extras such as Bluetooth and AirPort status as well as the day and time. Menu extras give you a quick way to view or adjust system information. For example, if you click the audio menu extra, you can adjust your Mac volume without having to open the System Preferences application.

Finally, in the far-right corner is the Spotlight menu (looks like a magnifying glass). Spotlight, Apple's built-in search technology, lets you find the files you want quickly and easily. I'll be covering Spotlight in more detail in the next chapter.

The Dock

Along the bottom of the window is the Dock. The Dock was first introduced with the original version of Mac OS X back in 2001 as a quick way to launch your most frequently used applications. Some have compared the Dock's functionality to that of the Windows Start menu, but I argue that the Dock is a much simpler launcher because it only focuses on your applications.

When you launch an application, it will appear in your Dock with a blue signal just below the icon to signify the application is open. When you quit an application, the blue signal disappears.

In addition to storing your applications, you can use the Dock to keep track of your files using **Stacks**, a feature new to Mac OS X Leopard that allows you to drag a group of files or folders into your Dock so you can quickly access them. The aim of Stacks is to reduce desktop clutter. By default, Apple includes a Stack called Downloads that contains all the files you download from Safari or attachments you save from Mail. You'll learn more about this feature in the section "Stacks" later in this chapter.

The desktop itself

On the surface of the desktop, you can place files and folders just like you would in any folder. The desktop itself is actually a folder in your home directory. In addition to the files you store on the desktop, Mac OS X also keeps an icon for the hard disk and any external disks you may have attached to your Mac. You can also see your iPod and any other networked volume you may have connected. If you'd rather not see a certain type of connection on your desktop, you can disable them by following these steps:

1. Click your desktop.

2. Click Finder in the menu bar and select Preferences.

3. In the Finder Preferences window, uncheck what type of connection you don't want shown on your desktop (see Figure 2-2).

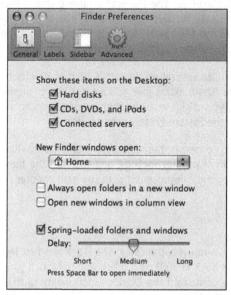

Figure 2-2. The Finder Preferences window allows you to specify which items may appear on your desktop.

Your desktop picture

The final piece to the desktop puzzle is your desktop background image. Whether it be a photograph of your kids from your personal collection or a cityscape you downloaded from the Internet, having a desktop background unique to you is part of what makes your Mac your own. Apple bundles several beautiful backdrops that you can use, or you can use your own photograph from iPhoto to give it a more personal touch. To change your background, follow these steps:

1. Click the Apple menu in the upper-left corner and select System Preferences.

2. In the System Preferences window, select Desktop & Screen Saver.

3. Click the image you'd like to use as your background.

Window elements

One of the great things about using a Mac is that it has a consistent user interface, so you don't have to adjust to several different ways of working with applications. If you've used Windows before, you've no doubt run into the problem of two different applications behaving completely differently: for example, one application may have a Close button in one place, while another may have it on the opposite side of the window.

That is not an issue with Mac OS X. At the top of any application or window, you will see four items.

1. The Close, Minimize, and Maximize buttons are located in the top-left corner of all windows. The colors mimic that of a stop light—red symbolizes closing a window, yellow minimizing, and green maximizing.

2. In the middle, you will see the window title or application name. If you are in an application like Microsoft Word, the title will be the document's name.

3. In the far-right corner is a small, white chiclet that will hide a window's toolbar.

4. The toolbar contains a set of frequently used actions you might perform in a given application. In Figure 2-3, you can see the Finder's toolbar. It has buttons to navigate forward and backward, toggle between the different views, use Quick Look, and access an Action menu, as well as a search pane for performing searches.

Figure 2-3. Each Mac OS X window has a set of common attributes.

The file system

Mac OS X is built on a powerful Unix foundation, which is part of what makes it so stable. Unix has been used as the backbone of many of the most powerful computers in the world because of its stability and power. Apple realized this when it set out to make its next-generation operating system.

Luckily, beyond this basic information, you don't need to know much more about the Unix power behind Mac OS X Leopard, because Apple keeps that information invisible from the Finder and the rest of the general Mac OS X system.

If you double-click the hard-drive icon on your desktop, you will notice four to five folders in the window that opens depending on your system (see Figure 2-4).

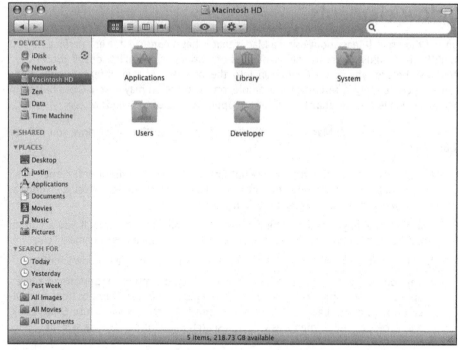

Figure 2-4. By default, Mac OS X only shows the system folders you need to see to work with your Mac.

- Applications: The Applications folder stores all the programs that come bundled with your Mac and also the ones you want to install.

- Developer: This is an optional folder used to store the developer tools employed to build Mac applications. If you are using a Mac in a corporate environment, you may see this folder, as many system administrators install the developer tools because it helps with debugging system problems.

- Library: The Library folder stores systemwide settings and preferences such as Spotlight importers, AppleScripts, and preference panes.

- System: The System folder is where the Mac OS X system information is stored. Here you will find system applications such as Finder and other pieces of Mac OS X that are essential to your system. However, 99% of the time you do not want to tinker with anything in this folder unless you are absolutely sure of what you are doing.

- Users: The Users folder is where each user's home directory is stored. For each unique Mac OS X login you create, that person gets his own directory to store his files and folders.

Besides the systemwide configuration, you should also take a look at the default configuration of your home folder. As I mentioned earlier, for each Mac OS X login, that person has her own unique home folder for storing personal files, photographs, music, and other items. The advantage of offering this on a per-user basis is that you can keep your financial documents on your personal account, for example, but your son can also use the Mac with his own login with no effect on that data. In fact, your son won't even have access to it.

If you click the Finder icon in the Dock, a new Finder window will appear with the default layout of your home directory (see Figure 2-5).

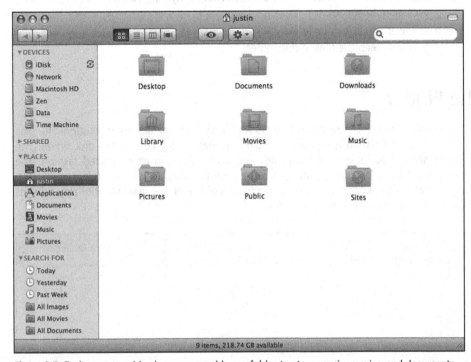

Figure 2-5. Each user on a Mac has a personal home folder to store music, movies, and documents.

In the home window, you will see nine different folders. Apple has created a folder for each type of document you may want to store.

- Desktop: This is where all the files that are stored on your desktop are placed.
- Documents: This is where you should store your documents, spreadsheets, and other personal files.
- Downloads: When you download a file from Safari or a Mail attachment, that file is saved to this folder by default.
- Library: Like the Library folder you saw before, this stores system configuration and settings information. The difference between the two Library folders is that the home directory one stores settings that are unique to each user. You usually don't want to save any files in the Library folder unless you are absolutely sure of what you are doing.
- Movies: This is where you would store any movies you download or make in iMovie.

- Music: By default, your iTunes library is stored in here. This includes any content you purchase from the iTunes store, rip from your personal CD collection, or gather from other means and import into iTunes.

- Pictures: This is where you would store any digital photographs or background images. Your iPhoto library is also kept in here by default.

- Public: This is a unique folder that is used to share files with other accounts on your Mac or other Macs on the same network. Anything you place in this folder is accessible to anyone.

- Sites: If you like to build web sites using iWeb or another web development solution, you keep the files in this folder.

The Finder

The Finder, shown in Figure 2-6, is Mac OS X's file and disk management solution. The Mac stores your information (programs and data) in files on the computer's disk drives. The Finder allows you to look at these files and access them in an organized fashion. The Finder has been a part of the Mac platform since the original Mac was released in 1984. While features have been added in each iteration of Finder, the main functionality remains the same: easy management of your files.

Figure 2-6. The Finder gives you a listing of the files and folders stored on your Mac.

The basic metaphor of file management that the Finder follows has been copied by many operating systems over the past 20 years, including Windows. Windows Explorer wouldn't be what it is today without the Finder. The basic notion is that your data is organized in files that are placed in **directories** (also called **folders**, because they look and act like folders). So you may have a folder that contains all of your documents. Within that, there may be a **subdirectory** that contains your personal files, another for your work files, and so on. In your personal files directory (folder), there may be subdirectories for word-processing documents, spreadsheets, photographs, and so on. The nested nature of the folders makes it simpler to find the file you are looking for, even if you don't know what it is called, when it was created, or by whom (the file's attributes). But, as you will see, you can search to find a file if you know at least one of its attributes.

Using the Finder can significantly improve your workflow. For instance, the Finder allows you to label any folder or file with a color so that you can visually recognize it. You can also save search result sets as a folder called a **smart folder**. This gives you quick access to your recently used documents from a single location. And speaking of quick access, no other operating system gives you a sidebar for your most frequently used folders and applications like the Finder does. I will be covering these topics (and more) in the following sections.

The Finder window

By default, the Finder window is separated into two sections, as you can see in Figure 2-7. The left side is known collectively as the **sidebar**. It starts with the heading of Devices, under which is a listing of the devices connected to your Mac such as hard disks, thumb drives, and iPods. The hard disk is the device that stores all of the data on your Mac. Most Macs come with a single drive, but if you have a Mac Pro, you may have more than one drive. If you attach an external FireWire or USB drive to your Mac, it will also appear under Devices.

Below Devices is the Shared section, which contains a listing of the other Macs that are available on your local network and any connected network volumes. If you have more than one Mac and want to access data on another machine, you can mount that machine's hard disk as a network volume. I'll be covering this in depth in Chapter 18.

Next is a listing of Places, which contains a customizable list of frequently used folders. By default, Apple includes your desktop, application, and several home directory folders. You can remove any of these folders by dragging them out of the window, and add or replace them with new folders by dragging the new folders into the area.

Finally, Apple includes a list of common Spotlight searches to help you find some of your most frequently used files.

The main portion of a Finder window gives you a listing of the files, folders, and applications in the currently selected directory. By default, these are shown as a set of free-form icons that you can move around anywhere in the Finder window. I'll discuss how to customize the layout of these files and folders later in the chapter.

Figure 2-7. By default, the Mac OS X Finder window gives a listing of network drives, hard disks, folders, and Spotlight search queries.

The Finder toolbar

You can customize the Finder's toolbar, shown in Figure 2-8, as you see fit. The default features include navigation arrows so you can jump between previously viewed folders; buttons to modify the window layout of your Finder window, use Quick Look, and access the Action menu; and search functionality. You can customize the buttons that are available in your toolbar easily.

1. Click your desktop.
2. In the menu bar, click the View menu.
3. Select Customize Toolbar.
4. A window will drop down in the active Finder window with a listing of the available icons.
5. Drag the icons you want to append onto the toolbar.

Figure 2-8. The Finder toolbar is customizable like many other portions of the Mac OS X interface.

In the following sections, I will describe what the items in the toolbar do.

The five views

I have already covered the default icon view that the Finder supports, but there are three other types of listings that you can use to view your files. If you click the silver chiclet in the upper-right corner of the window, the sidebar and toolbar will be hidden, and you will see only a listing of your files and folders, as shown in Figure 2-9. This minimalist view is often seen in a disk image that is downloaded with a shareware application from the Web. Clicking the chiclet icon again will revert the window back to a standard window style.

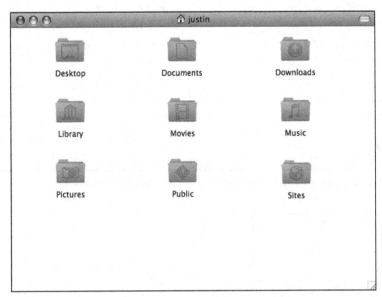

Figure 2-9. The minimalist Finder window view removes the sidebar and toolbar from a Finder window.

To switch between the other three types of views, you choose from a set of four buttons that are next to the navigational arrows in the Finder toolbar. The far-left button is for the default free-form icon view.

Clicking the button with four horizontal lines will transform the window into a list view (see Figure 2-10). The list view shows you the file name, the date it was modified, the size of the file, and what type of file it is. You can modify the columns that are displayed by going to the View menu and selecting Show View Options to bring up the options shown in Figure 2-11.

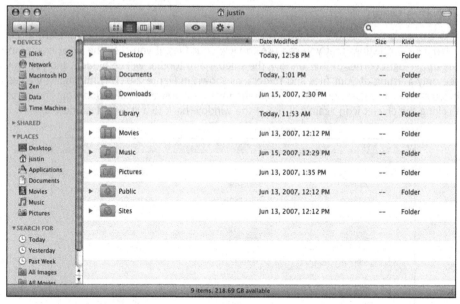

Figure 2-10. The Finder list view lets you view and sort your files and folders easily.

Figure 2-11.
The view options let you manipulate the columns, icon size, and text size of a Finder window.

Besides the columns to display, you can also decide whether to show a small or large icon, the size of text, how to display dates, and whether to also show the size of the files contained in a folder.

Clicking the view button with three vertical rectangles switches your window to column view (see Figure 2-12). Column view displays several vertical columns that list the currently selected folder as well as its parent folders. Column view makes it easy to move files between folders. Clicking a specific file in column view also gives you information and a preview of the file.

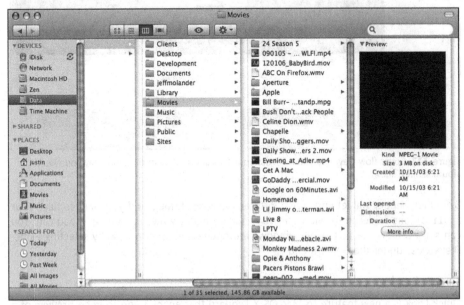

Figure 2-12. Column view lets you quickly navigate through folders and see the hierarchy of your Mac's file system.

Clicking the far-right view button in the Finder toolbar exposes you to cover flow view (see Figure 2-13). This view, new to Mac OS X Leopard, lets you browse your files much in the same way you would browser album art in iTunes. Each file is represented by a larger icon than in the other views. If you are looking at pictures, you will see a preview of the actual image.

Figure 2-13. Cover flow view lets you navigate your files and folders in the same way you would album art in iTunes.

By default, Finder will let you save a different view per folder, so if you want to have your Applications folder in list view and your home directory files in icon view, you can. You can set a preference so that all windows are opened in column view by selecting Finder Preferences under the Finder menu.

Quick Look

Quick Look is a new feature to Mac OS X Leopard that enables you to get a preview of a file without having to open the application that created it. For example, if you want to preview a Word document or PDF, you can select it in the Finder and click the Quick Look button to see the contents of the file (see Figure 2-14). Quick Look saves you the time of having to wait for the application to load up just to ensure that the file you are opening is what you are looking for.

To activate Quick Look, click the Quick Look button (the one with an eye icon) in the Finder's toolbar. A translucent black window will appear on your screen with the preview of the file or folder you want to look at.

Quick Look works with most major file types by default, and Mac developers have the option of adding support for Quick Look into their applications by using technology provided to them by Apple.

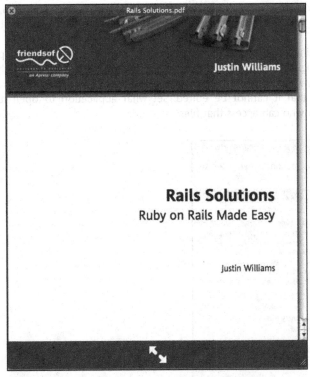

Figure 2-14. Quick Look enables you to preview files without even opening the application that created them.

The Action menu

In Mac OS X 10.3 Panther, Apple introduced the Action menu as the single source for the main actions that you can perform in a Finder window. You can easily recognize it by its gear icon (see Figure 2-15). Clicking it lets you perform one of several actions.

Figure 2-15.
The Action menu lets you perform several actions in relation to your files and folders.

23

From the Action menu, you can create folders, get information on your files, copy files, or apply labels to folders. Let's take a look at some of the more interesting options.

Get Info Clicking a file or folder and then selecting Get Info will open up a secondary window (see Figure 2-16) that will give you as much information about that file as the system can show you. Beyond the basic metadata, the Get Info option lets you set a label, lock a file so that it cannot be edited, set what application to open it with, or set permissions for who can access that file.

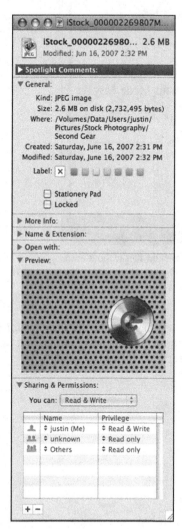

Figure 2-16.
Get Info gives you information about a file and, where available, a preview of the file.

In the case of an image or a movie file, you can also get a preview of that file so you can quickly view it from there.

Compress 2 Items Mac OS X includes built-in support for compressing files and folders as ZIP files. After selecting the items you want to compress, go to the Action menu and select Compress 2 Items. If you have selected a single file, it will name the ZIP archive after that file. If you select more than one file or folder, it will by default name the archive Archive.zip.

You can rename the file by clicking the file's name once, typing in the new file name, and pressing the Return key.

Make Alias If you want to make a shortcut to a folder in another place such as your desktop or another folder, you can select that folder or file and select Make Alias. You can then drag that alias anywhere on your system. You can always tell an alias from an actual file or folder by the small arrow in the lower-left corner of the icon (see Figure 2-17). If you click the alias, it will open the original file.

Figure 2-17.
Aliases can be put anywhere so you can quickly get to a file or folder.

Label Any file, folder, or alias can have a label associated with it (see Figure 2-18). A label allows you to assign a visual cue to a file so that your eye is drawn to it more easily. Many people use different colors on labels to notate the context for a file. For example, I use a red label to mark any file or folder that I think is super important. I use a yellow label for marking files that I frequently access.

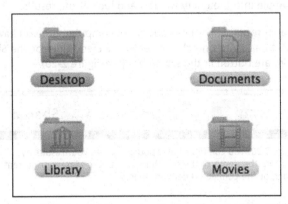

Figure 2-18. Labels let you set a visual cue for your files or folders.

Labels have been a part of the Mac OS experience since the Classic OS days. When you click the Action menu, the Label section shows seven different colors that you can select. When you hover over one of the colors, the name of that label will show below it. Clicking one of the colors will modify the background color of the file's name to match the color of the label.

When you hover over a label's color in the Action menu, the name of the label appears below it. By default, these labels are named after the color it represents. You can modify the name of these labels in the Finder Preferences window (see Figure 2-19).

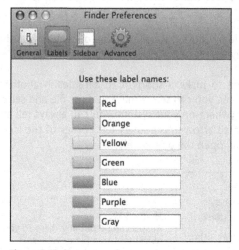

Figure 2-19. You can assign a custom name to each label.

Search

The last part of the default toolbar is a search pane that lets you search the contents of your computer. The Finder uses Apple's Spotlight technology to do the searching. I'll be covering Spotlight more in the next chapter, but if you want to get a feel for how it works, give it a try: type **Apple** into the query window and look at the results.

By default, the search results will query your entire computer, but you have the option of filtering the search to apply to only the currently selected folder or the Shared folder by clicking the appropriate button in the search bar (see Figure 2-20).

Figure 2-20. You can filter how Spotlight shows your results by adjusting the depth of the search to your entire Mac, your current folder, or the connected network shares.

Smart folders

When you perform a search in a Finder window, a Save button appears in the upper-right corner, as shown in Figure 2-21. Clicking this button will allow you to save the search result as a smart folder. Like in iTunes, smart folders give you quick access to the results of your search. Also like in iTunes, you can add different criteria to the search by clicking the Add button (the button with the + sign) to the right of the Save button.

Figure 2-21. The smart folder feature lets you create a folder that stores a Spotlight query that you often reference.

When you save your folder, it will be saved in the Saved Searches folder located in your home directory's Library folder. You also have the option to put the smart folder in your sidebar for quick access from any Finder window. Mac OS X will automatically place it in the Search For section of the sidebar.

Spring-loaded folders

One feature of the Mac OS X Finder that is unmatched in any other operating system is **spring-loaded folders**, which provide a way to quickly navigate through folders when you want to move files or folders around your system. To use spring-loaded folders, click and drag a file or folder and hover it over another folder. Watch as the folder you are hovering over automatically opens up.

You can then drop the folder in that folder or hover over subsequent folders and watch them spring open until you find the folder you want to drop your file into. After you have dropped your file or folder into its destination folder, all the other folders will automatically close so that you aren't left with a messy desktop.

There is a short delay before a folder springs open, but you can modify the length of that delay by going to the Finder Preferences window and modifying the Delay option at the bottom of the General section.

> *You can also instantly open a folder you are hovering over by pressing the spacebar.*

Working with files

Now that you know the basics of how to work with the Finder, how do you go about actually working with your files?

Creating folders

There are two different ways to create folders in the Finder. The first is to go to the File menu and select New Folder (see Figure 2-22). The second is to click the Action menu on any Finder window and select New Folder. Either performs the same action—it creates a new folder in the currently selected Finder window.

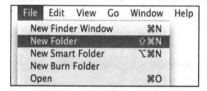

Figure 2-22. You can create a new folder from either the File menu or any Finder window's Action menu.

Moving and copying files and folders

Moving a file or folder is as simple as clicking the file and dragging it to the folder you want to store it in.

Copying a file is different from moving the file in that it makes a second version of the file that you can keep on the Mac. When I want to make a lot of large changes to a file, I tend to back up the original before I go about making those changes. If I am not happy with the modifications I made, I can just delete the changed file and keep the original copy I made.

Copying a file is as easy as going to the File menu or Action menu and selecting Copy. This will create a copy of the file in the same folder as the original. You can then rename and move the file as necessary.

Deleting files and folders

If you look at the far-right end of your Dock, you will see the trashcan icon, as shown in Figure 2-23. The trashcan stores files and folders you no longer want.

Figure 2-23.
The trashcan is where you put files that you
no longer want to keep on your Mac.

There are two different ways to delete a file in the Finder. The first involves using the File
or Action menus and selecting Move To Trash.

After you move a file to the trash, you can empty the trash by going to the Finder menu
and selecting Empty Trash (see Figure 2-24). If you find that you accidentally put a file in
the trash that you didn't want to, you can remove it by clicking the trashcan icon in your
Dock and removing the file from the trash folder.

Figure 2-24.
Empty Trash removes all the files that
you have put in your trashcan.

Stacks

Stacks, which are new to Mac OS X Leopard, make it easy to organize and work with a
group of files or applications that you often access. Stacks appear in the Dock as a collection of files on top of each other. The most recently added item will appear on top of the
Stack.

Clicking a Stack displays each of the files in the Stack in an arc (see Figure 2-25).

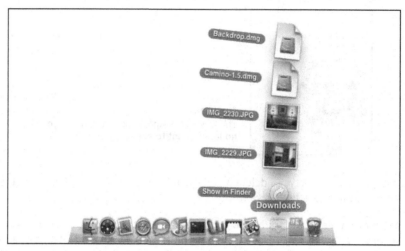

Figure 2-25. A small Stack displays the contents in an elegant arc.

If you have a large number of files in a Stack, Leopard will organize them in a grid (see Figure 2-26).

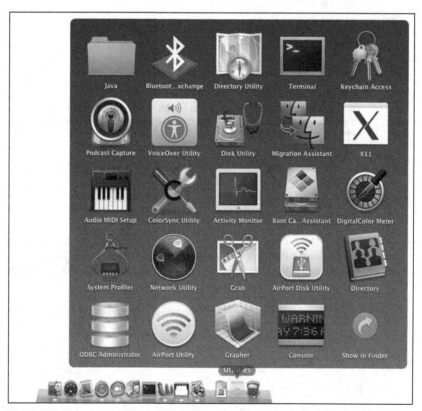

Figure 2-26. If you have a large number of items in your Stack, they will display in a grid pattern.

There are several different ways you can create a Stack. The easiest is to just drag a folder from a Finder window onto the Dock to the left of the trashcan. A space will slide open that allows you to drop the folder into the Dock.

The second way to create a Stack is to highlight several items by holding down the Option key while you click each file or folder you want added to your Stack. Once you are satisfied with your selections, click one of the items and hold your mouse down as you drag the collection to your Dock.

If you want to remove a Stack from your Dock, just drag it out of the Dock. The Stack will slide out of the Dock and disappear.

Installing applications

Installing applications on the Mac is much easier than installing software on most other platforms, but it can be confusing to new Mac users at first. The basic premise for installing Mac OS X software is acquire, unpackage, and install.

Acquire

Your Mac comes with a lot of great software such as iChat, iPhoto, and Safari, but there may be times when you need a piece of software that doesn't come bundled with Mac OS X Leopard. The best place to find Mac software is MacUpdate (www.macupdate.com) or VersionTracker (www.versiontracker.com). Both sites give a listing of all the software that is available for Mac OS X and are updated several times a day with the newest releases.

In addition to downloading software, you can also purchase copies from several retail stores such as Apple's official retail stores, CompUSA, or Fry's.

> For more information on Mac software, check out Appendix A.

Unpackage

Before any software can be installed, it must first be unpackaged. If you are installing from a CD you purchased or some other kind of disk, you can generally just insert the disk into your machine, and move on to the next section.

If you download your software from the Web, you will usually receive it in one of three types of files: ZIP, StuffIt, or a disk image (DMG) file. ZIP and DMG files are handled natively by Mac OS X, but decompressing a StuffIt archive requires the third-party StuffIt software from Allume (www.stuffit.com/mac/expander/). Most software is distributed by ZIP or DMG now, but there are still a few developers such as Microsoft that use StuffIt.

When working with a ZIP or StuffIt archive, you can unpackage a file you download by double-clicking it and waiting for OS X to open it.

Disk images work a bit differently. Think of a DMG as a virtual CD that you download from the Web. When you double-click it, it will mount as if it were another drive or disk on your Mac. You can see it in the Finder's sidebar, as shown in Figure 2-27.

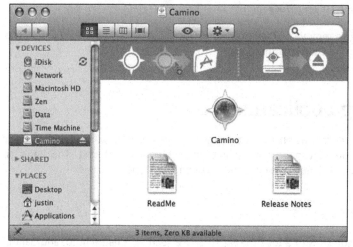

Figure 2-27. When you double-click a disk image, it appears in the Finder's sidebar as a virtual drive on your Mac.

Install

The final step to the process is actually installing the software you want to use. Software developers usually choose one of two different methods for installing an application—manually dragging and dropping files or using an installer.

In the case of the Camino application you saw in Figure 2-27, you can install the application by dragging the Camino icon into your Mac's Applications folder.

More complex applications such as a Mac OS X system update are installed by an installer. To run an installer, just double-click the installer icon (see Figure 2-28) and follow the onscreen instructions.

Figure 2-28.
You can easily detect an installer by the open box icon that represents it.

Whether you install an application via drag and drop or an installer, the final destination is the Applications folder. Double-clicking the application inside that folder will launch it and allow you to use it.

Burning disks

You can burn data disks from the Finder easily. There are two ways to go about burning a disk: you can perform a one-time burn or use a burn folder for those files you want to burn more than once.

One-time burns

If you want to quickly create a disk just once, insert your media in your Mac's burner. A window will pop up asking you what type of disk you want to burn. You can select whether to open the disk in the Finder, iTunes, or Disk Utility. Finder is selected by default.

A disk will appear on your desktop that you can then drag files and folders onto. Once you have put all the data on the disk you want, you can double-click the disk and then click Burn to begin the burn session.

Burn folders

If you have a common set of files that you need to burn more than once, the best way to burn them is to create a **burn folder**. A burn folder is identifiable by the biohazard logo on its side (see Figure 2-29).

Burn Folder

Figure 2-29.
A burn folder has a biohazard logo on it.

Like burning a single disk, all you do is drag the files and folders you want to burn into the burn folder and then select the Burn button in the upper-right corner.

Since a burn folder is saved on your disk, you can go back to it and burn it again at any point in time. You can also add and remove files as you see fit.

Summary

After reading this chapter, you should have a solid foundation of Mac OS X knowledge that you can build on throughout the rest of the book. This chapter covered a lot of ground. I introduced the basics of Mac OS X in terms of window styles, common interface elements, and how to work with the Finder. I showed you how to work with files and folders and install applications as well.

In the next chapter, you will start building on this knowledge by learning about Spotlight, Apple's powerful search technology.

3 SPOTLIGHT

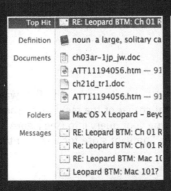

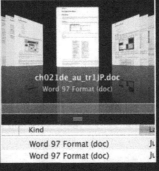

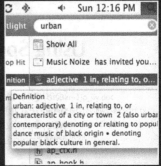

Spotlight is Mac OS X's systemwide search solution introduced in Mac OS X Tiger. Spotlight expands traditional searching by not only searching file names, but also searching the contents of each document. Spotlight can search text files, images, e-mails, calendars, and more. Developers can even integrate their applications with Spotlight using the Apple-provided application programming interfaces (APIs).

In addition to indexing the title and contents of a file, Spotlight is also capable of importing metadata. **Metadata** includes the file type, date modified, size, author, and more. One example of metadata is in digital photographs. Each time you shoot a photo with your digital camera, the photo embeds information about the aperture, shutter speed, type of camera used, and more inside the file. This data, called **EXIF data**, is a form of metadata. Spotlight keeps all of the metadata of your files inside the **Spotlight data store** that runs in the background of your Mac. The Spotlight store is constantly keeping track of changes to your files and file system and importing any changes that you may make. With this information, Spotlight can quickly search it as if it were your own personal Google.

Setting up Spotlight

Since Spotlight is built into Mac OS X Leopard, the initial setup process is drop-dead simple.

When you launch your Mac for the first time, Spotlight begins indexing your hard drive. **Indexing** is the process of importing the metadata from all of the files and folders on your hard drive into the Spotlight database. By importing this data into a database, Spotlight can more quickly retrieve and display your results. If the content weren't indexed in a database like the store, you would be waiting quite a while to search through several gigabytes of files.

Indexing your hard drive can take anywhere from 30 minutes to several hours depending on how much data is stored on your drive. You can tell when Spotlight is indexing by looking at the magnifying glass icon in the top-right corner. If the inside of the magnifying glass icon is pulsating, Spotlight is indexing data.

Using Spotlight

Spotlight is easy to use no matter what application you are in. The first way to access Spotlight is via the menu item in the upper-right corner of the menu bar. When clicked, a small text input field will appear that you can type your query into (see Figure 3-1). As you type, Spotlight has already begun searching the Spotlight store for any data that matches your criteria.

The search results are returned in an organized listing based on the category of data shown. At the top of the list is the file that Spotlight thinks most matches the criteria you have given it. Below that is a summary of files sorted by documents, folders, e-mail messages, events, images, and PDFs. If you don't happen to see the exact file you were looking for in this quick results window, clicking Show All will open up a window that gives you a full listing of your results (see Figure 3-2), much the same as what you'd see when searching directly from the Finder. You can also sort and filter your data even more with the modifiers available below the toolbar.

Spotlight is also enabled in certain applications. For example, the search bar in a Finder window searches the Spotlight data store. When you save a file in an application like TextEdit or iChat, it will also have a search bar that is powered by Spotlight.

Third-party applications are also able to use Spotlight as their search query provider. For example, NetNewsWire, the popular RSS reader for the Mac, uses Spotlight to search through the contents of all your RSS feeds. In addition to the in-application Spotlight search, you can also use the global Spotlight query window to get results from NetNewsWire.

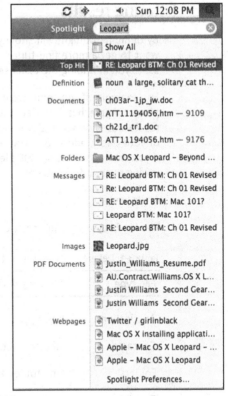

Figure 3-1.
Spotlight separates your data by the types of files it is showing.

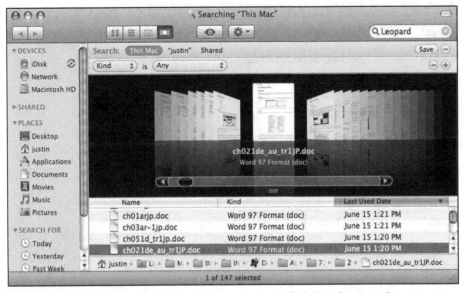

Figure 3-2. The Spotlight results window gives you a more detailed view of your results.

Filtering results

By default, Spotlight will show you the results for all file types that it understands. If you want to get a more fine-tuned results set, Apple has included a set of keywords that can assist you in finding the exact set of data you need.

For example, if you only wanted to show a listing of PDFs that referenced a word or phrase, Apple has included the **kind** keyword. Using this keyword, you can filter your results based on whether the results are applications, images, movies, or more. At the end of your query, add kind:*type* where *type* is the type of file you want to show. For example, if you wanted to find all PDF files that contained the word *Apple*, you would enter the following query into Spotlight:

Apple kind:pdf

The kind keyword supports the file types shown in Table 3-1.

Table 3-1. Default file types supported by keywords

File type	Kind keyword listing
Applications	kind:application, kind:app, kind:applications
Contacts	kind:contact, kind:contacts
Folders	kind:folder, kind:folders
E-mail	kind:email, kind:emails, kind:mail message, kind:mail messages
iCal events	kind:event, kind:events
iCal to-dos	kind:todo, kind:todos, kind:to do, kind:to dos
Images	kind:images, kind:image
Movies	kind:movie, kind:movies
Music	kind:music
Audio	kind:audio
PDF	kind:pdf, kind:pdfs
Preferences	kind:system preferences, kind:preferences
Bookmarks	kind:bookmark, kind:bookmarks
Fonts	kind:font, kind:fonts
Presentations	kind:presentation, kind:presentations

Besides filtering by the kind of document, you can also filter by dates. If you know you edited a file in the past week, you can filter your Spotlight results accordingly. Like the kind keyword, the date keyword is appended to your Spotlight query like so:

kind:PDF date:last week

This query would search Spotlight for all PDFs that were opened or created last week. For a complete list of available date keywords, see Table 3-2.

Table 3-2. Date keywords

Date	Date keyword listing
Today	date:today
Yesterday	date:yesterday
Tomorrow	date:tomorrow
This week	date:this week
This month	date:this month
This year	date:this year
Next week	date:next week
Next month	date:next month
Next year	date:next year

Mac OS X Leopard includes support for more advanced queries using Boolean logic. **Boolean logic** lets you use keywords such as AND, OR, and NOT to further filter your search results. Using AND, you can string together a set of queries so that all of the criteria must match for the result to appear. If you had two dogs, Cali and Romeo, but only wanted to see pictures of Cali, you could use AND logic to query Spotlight for dog AND Cali type:picture. Using OR logic, you can get results that match one or more of the criteria. For example, with the query dog OR Cali type:picture, you'd get your dog results, but you might also get photos of California that you may have on your hard drive.

Finally, the NOT keyword lets you filter what you *don't* want to be shown in your results. For example, you could find all instances of dog photos that aren't Yorkies by typing a query like Dog NOT Yorkie type:picture

Besides the Boolean logic, there is also a new keyword to filter results by: **author**. You can now show only results for files that are created by a certain person. For example, you can get a listing of all PDFs created by Robert Reid by using type:pdf author:Robert Reid.

Privacy

By default, Spotlight will index everything that is on your machine (save for the Unix underpinnings), but you are able to restrict what folders Spotlight doesn't index in the System Preferences' Spotlight pane. If you were sharing your hard drive over the network but didn't want sensitive data like your financial documents to appear in any Spotlight searches, you would want to hide the folders that contain this data from the Spotlight store.

To do this, follow these steps.

1. Open the System Preferences application.

2. Click the Spotlight icon.

3. Select the Privacy tab.

4. In the Privacy tab, click the plus (+) button to open a folder selector (see Figure 3-3).

5. Select the folder you want to hide. Repeat these steps for each folder you want to restrict.

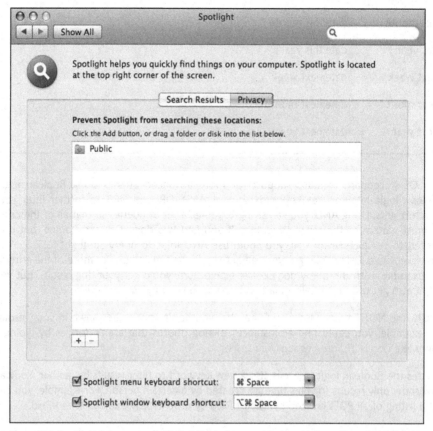

Figure 3-3. Spotlight lets you explicitly tell the indexer not to keep information about files in certain folders.

Quick Look

When you view your Spotlight results in a separate window, you can use the new Quick Look feature to look at an image or a document instantly. The selected item will appear in a semitranslucent overlay (see Figure 3-4). If you open a QuickTime movie in Quick Look, you can even play it from there.

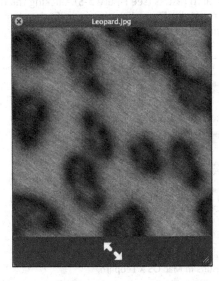

Figure 3-4.
The Quick Look feature introduced in Mac OS X Leopard gives you a way to easily look at certain file types without having to open another application.

To view a file in Quick Look, follow these steps:

1. Control-click (right-click) the file you are interested in previewing.

2. Select Quick Look.

By default, Apple supports images, presentations, documents, and movies, but third-party developers can also add support for Quick Look into their applications. If an application is not supported by Quick Look, only the icon will appear in the Quick Look panel.

> *In addition to Quick Look working in the* Spotlight *window, it is also available in the Finder from any window by clicking the* eye *icon.*

Remote search

You can also search remote servers using Spotlight in Mac OS X Leopard. Any Mac on your home network that has Personal File Sharing enabled will be indexed in your local Spotlight store so you can access that information in your search results. The results will turn up files from remote systems just as if they were on your local Mac. When you are ready to access the files, all you need to do is access the remote server, and it will show up on your local machine.

Tips and tricks

Apple included a few nice enhancements to make Spotlight useful beyond just showing search results. For example, you can use Spotlight to get a word's definition from the system's dictionary. If you search for the word *Urban* in Spotlight, it will show any file that references the word *Urban*, but it will also show you the dictionary definition. The definition will appear inline with the rest of your search results (see Figure 3-5). Clicking the definition will open the word in the Dictionary application where you can find out more about its etymology or find similar words using the thesaurus.

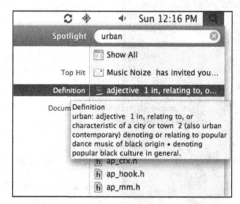

Figure 3-5. Dictionary definitions are included in your Spotlight search results in Mac OS X Leopard.

In addition to dictionary support, Spotlight can also perform basic math operations. In the past, I would open the system's calculator application to do some quick math calculations. With Mac OS X Leopard, I can now just type the query into Spotlight, and the calculator will display the results in the results window.

Besides addition, subtraction, multiplication, and division, you can also use functions like log, tan, sqrt, and pi (see Figure 3-6).

Figure 3-6. You can perform basic mathematic functions in Spotlight now.

Any function that is available in the Mac OS X calculator application can be performed in a Spotlight query window in Mac OS X Leopard.

Summary

In this chapter, I covered the basics of using Spotlight, Mac OS X's systemwide search technology. I showed you how Spotlight indexes your files, how you can perform basic queries, and how you can preview your files using Quick Look. You also saw how to restrict certain information from appearing in your Spotlight results using the built-in privacy features, and you learned some tips and tricks that make Spotlight even more useful.

The next chapter covers Apple's Mail application and how Mac OS X Leopard makes it easy to read and respond to messages from your friends and family.

3

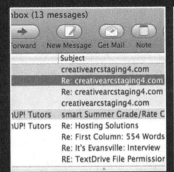  

There's no doubt that e-mail has changed the way we communicate with friends, family, and coworkers. What used to require a stamp and a few days to transmit can now be sent instantly via the Internet and an e-mail client. Sharing photos, family news, and other types of data has become seamless thanks to e-mail. Apple has bundled a powerful mail client called Mail (or Mail.app) that takes its roots from the NeXTStep origins of Mac OS X. Over the years, Apple has improved Mail's functionality, but never so much as it has in Mac OS X Leopard. Apple has bundled support for storing notes and tasks in addition to your e-mail messages in Mail. It also added support for reading RSS feeds in Mail in addition to Safari.

Before getting into those new features, let's take a look at some of the standard e-mail features of Mail.

Setting up Mail

If you have a .Mac account, the mail settings for the associated e-mail account will be automatically set up when you first launch Mail. If you have other mail accounts to configure, those are all handled in Mail's preferences window under the Accounts tab. You can access Mail's preferences from the menu bar by selecting Mail ➤ Preferences. In the window that pops up, click the Accounts button, followed by the plus (+) button at the bottom of the window.

When you add an account, a wizard will open that walks you through the account creation process (see Figure 4-1). Mail supports IMAP, POP3, and Microsoft Exchange e-mail accounts. Each of these is a different type of server connection you can use to connect to your e-mail account. You can get connection details from either your Internet service provider or company's system administrator.

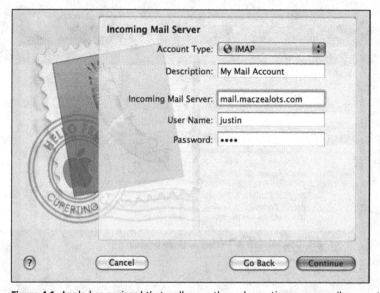

Figure 4-1. Apple has a wizard that walks you through creating your e-mail account.

Once you have entered your account's server settings in the wizard, you can then customize the settings in the Accounts tab. Select the account you want to edit, and you'll see three tabs in the window, as shown in Figure 4-2: Account Information, Mailbox Behaviors, and Advanced.

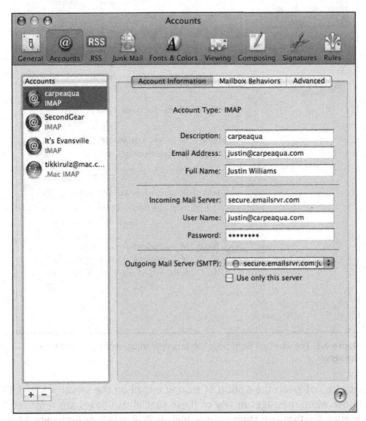

Figure 4-2. The Account Information tab lets you edit e-mail address and server information.

The Account Information tab lets you adjust the e-mail address and server information for the account you are using. You can also adjust the how your name will appear—if you don't want your real name to be sent with your e-mail, for example—with the e-mail by changing what's in the Full Name field.

The Mailbox Behaviors tab (see Figure 4-3) controls what Mail does with drafts, sent mail, junk mail, notes, to-do lists, and trash messages. If you are working with a .Mac, IMAP, or Exchange account, you can opt to store your Mail data on the e-mail server rather than locally on your Mac. This is a good idea if you are using more than one Mac, or if you want to ensure that there is always a backup of all your e-mail.

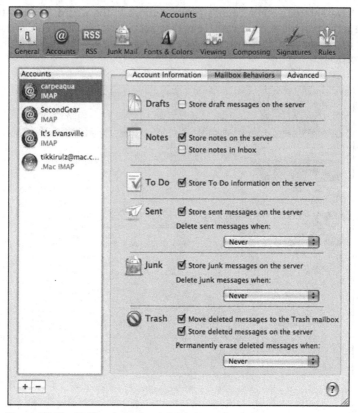

Figure 4-3. The Mailbox Behaviors tab lets you adjust what you store on the server.

POP accounts are not given the option of storing e-mail on the server. Instead, POP users can only choose when messages in any of these special mailboxes are removed from the server. No matter whether you store your e-mail via POP, IMAP, or Exchange, Mail caches a local copy of your e-mail so you can view it while offline.

The Advanced tab (see Figure 4-4) lets you enable or disable a specific e-mail account and whether or not to use SSL when connecting to your servers. **SSL** is a secure way to connect to your e-mail server.

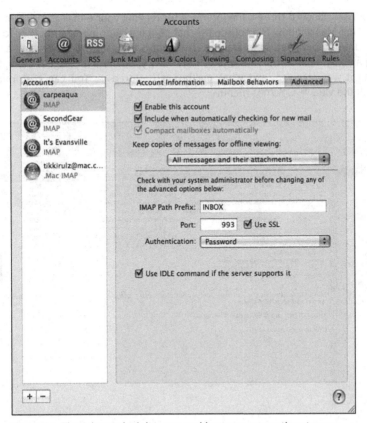

Figure 4-4. The Advanced tab lets you enable secure connections to your
e-mail via SSL and choose whether to automatically check for messages.

Usually, you won't need to access this information unless you are instructed to by your system administrator or Internet service provider.

Of interest to some is Leopard's new support for IDLE when working with IMAP accounts. **IDLE** is an option extension that your server may have enabled that allows the server to send new message updates to Mail in real time. In other words, as soon as a message is sent to your inbox, you will be notified. This technology, known as **push technology**, is common on devices such as BlackBerrys. Check with your e-mail provider to see if it supports IDLE.

Reading e-mail

You have no doubt read e-mail in one or more applications before, and Mail doesn't really offer any sort of groundbreaking e-mail functionality that is not found in other e-mail clients. What it does offer, however, is a fully streamlined reading setup that allows you to quickly search, filter, and organize your e-mail.

Mail supports a standard three-pane interface for reading your e-mail (see Figure 4-5). On the left of the Mail window is a source list that contains your inbox and other folders for each account you have set up in Mail. On the right is the list of messages and a message preview pane. By default, the message listing shows you who a message is from, the subject, when it was received, and what mailbox it is stored in. You can customize these columns in the View ➤ Columns menu.

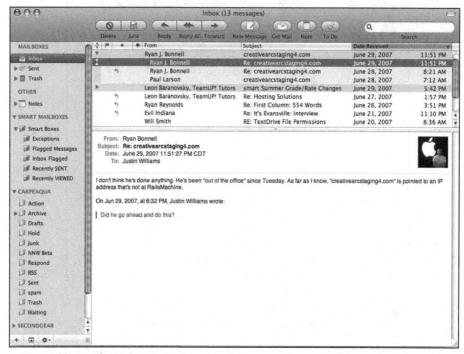

Figure 4-5. Apple's Mail uses a familiar three-pane interface to display a user's e-mail.

The message preview pane is a WebKit view. **WebKit** is browser-rendering engine that powers Safari. By using WebKit to display e-mail messages, Mail is able to render HTML e-mails the same as Safari or any other browser would. Unlike Safari, Mail has disabled WebKit's support for JavaScript to prevent a malicious script inside an e-mail from executing.

I will cover the power of HTML e-mail later in this chapter in the section "Stationery."

> *If you prefer reading each message in a separate window, you can hide the message preview pane by double-clicking the separator between the message list and the preview pane.*

Threads

If you are carrying on a long conversation over e-mail, it can be difficult to keep all of those e-mails organized in your inbox. Mail has built-in support for message threading. **Threading** groups all messages with the same subject together, as shown in Figure 4-6.

		●	✐	From	Subject	Date Received	
▼				Jim Geiser	[SPAM] Re: South Western I...	Today	8:57 AM
			↰	Jim Geiser	[SPAM] Re: South Western I...	Today	8:57 AM
		↰		Jim Geiser	[SPAM] Re: South Western I...	Today	8:57 AM
		↰		Jim Geiser	South Western Indiana PC ...	Yesterday	5:06 PM

Figure 4-6. By threading messages, you are able to organize like messages so they are easy to find in your inbox.

To enable threading, go to the View menu and select Organize By Thread. You can define whether you want to organize messages by thread on a per-folder basis.

The real power of working with threads is when used in conjunction with your keyboard. Using the left and right arrow keys, you can quickly expand and collapse threads without ever having to touch your mouse.

Long headers

Since the invention of e-mail, Apple and other e-mail client providers have worked to simplify the interface of their respective clients. One of the ways they improved usability is by condensing message headers to only the bare necessities: whom a message is from, to whom it was sent, when it was sent, and a subject. Even though this is the only data that is shown by default, Mail also keeps some other information about each e-mail you send and receive. For example, each e-mail you receive also includes the exact path it took through the servers between the sender and yourself (see Figure 4-7).

Figure 4-7. Long headers give you the full skinny about the e-mail you send and receive.

This data, among others, is collectively known as the **long headers** of a message. You can access this information from within Mail by going to the View menu and selecting Message ▶ Long Headers. Long headers appear on a per-message basis, so make sure you have only a single message selected and not a thread.

Besides showing and hiding long headers, the Message menu also lets you determine how a message is rendered. By default, Apple tries to render a message using WebKit's HTML rendering, but you can also show the raw source of a message by selecting Raw Source from the View ➤ Message window. This will render the selected message without any inline images, font styling, or other niceties that HTML-rendered e-mail can offer. In fact, if you try to render an e-mail that has an embedded image with raw source, you will see nothing but garbled text where the image would be, as shown in Figure 4-8.

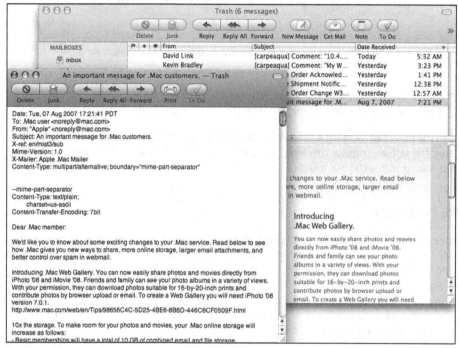

Figure 4-8. Rendering a message as raw source not only removes the styling of a message, but also renders images as text.

Dealing with spam

Spam is an unavoidable evil when it comes to working with e-mail. No matter how hard we try to prevent it from reaching our inboxes, it always seems to find a way there. Luckily, Apple has bundled a powerful antispam engine in Mail. Mail uses Bayesian filtering to determine what messages it thinks are spam. Mail is so good at detecting this spam, it has been lauded for its greater than 95 percent accuracy rate. Mail's success formula for detecting spam is twofold: while it does include a set of default behaviors that make it excel at detecting a spam message, it also allows users to train the spam engine to detect what is and isn't junk mail.

By default, most spam engines will think that an e-mail containing information about home mortgages is spam, but if you are in the market for such a thing and legitimately asked to receive e-mail messages about mortgages, you may not want Mail to mark those messages as junk. When you mark them as not junk (see Figure 4-9), Mail learns this behavior and will not mark future messages that are similar as junk.

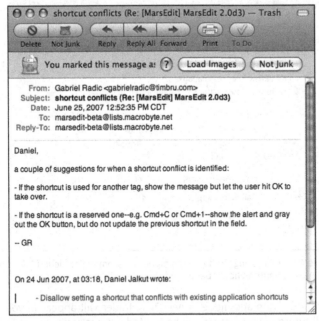

Figure 4-9. Mail marks messages it thinks are junk with a brown overlay and a snazzy trash bag.

If your mail server supports SpamAssassin or Brightmail, Mail can work with those solutions to further filter your e-mail from junk mail. See your ISP or system administrator for more information.

When you first start using Mail, it begins with its junk mail system in training mode. **Training mode** is beneficial because it lets Mail learn what you think is and isn't junk mail from the beginning. While in training mode, all messages will appear in your inbox whether they are marked as junk or not. Junk messages will be identified by the brown paper bag and overlay at the top of the message as shown in Figure 4-9. If you notice a message is marked as junk, but it really is legitimate mail, mark it as not junk by clicking the Not Junk button. If, on the other hand, a junk message isn't marked as such, you can click the Junk button in the Mail toolbar to identify it as spam.

Once you are satisfied with Mail's spam detection accuracy, you can switch from training mode to **automatic mode**. To switch to automatic mode, perform the following steps:

1. Open Mail's preferences window.

2. Select the Junk Mail tab.

3. Under When junk mail arrives, click the Move it to the Junk mailbox radio button option (see Figure 4-10).

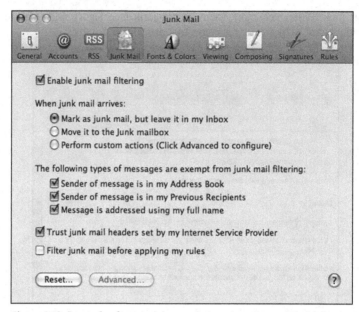

Figure 4-10. By moving from training mode to automatic mode in Mail, your junk mail will automatically be filtered to a Junk mailbox.

When you switch to automatic mode, a new Junk folder will appear in your folders list. This is where all future junk messages will be located automatically.

> If you find that Mail doesn't offer as much customization of your spam filtering as you'd like, you might want to check out the shareware application SpamSieve from C-Command (http://c-command.com/spamsieve/).

Organizing your mail

As you receive more and more e-mail, you may find that keeping everything in your inbox is neither manageable nor functional. Mail supports the use of folders for storing your messages. You can manually create a folder that can hold important e-mails by going to the Mailbox menu and selecting New Mailbox. For some reason, Mail calls each folder a mailbox even though the icon that appears in your sidebar is a folder. I digress.

When you select the New Mailbox option, a pane appears that lets you name your new mailbox and decide where to store it. If you only want to keep the information locally, select On your Mac. If you'd like the mailbox to be synchronized across multiple machines, store it on your mail server.

Mail supports subfolders for even more fine-grained organization of your messages. You can turn any mailbox into a subfolder by dragging it into another folder.

Besides manually managing your mail with mailboxes, you can also create **smart mailboxes** that will aggregate your e-mail based on predefined rules that you define. To create a smart mailbox, select New Smart Mailbox from the Mailbox menu. Creating a smart mailbox follows the exact same workflow as creating a smart folder in the Finder, which you learned in Chapter 2.

Unlike regular mailboxes, smart mailboxes are stored locally only. If you have a .Mac account, they can be synchronized across multiple Macs, but they cannot be stored on a Mail server. If you find that you have a lot of smart mailboxes, you can organize them in a smart mailbox folder. You can create that by selecting New Smart Mailbox folder under the Mailbox menu.

Filtering

4

If you subscribe to mailing lists or like to organize messages associated with your job separately from your personal messages, Mail's powerful filtering system will allow you to work with Mail more effectively. A **filter** is a way of sorting and organizing your e-mail based on a set of rules you provide. Filters are created and managed in the Mail preferences window's Rules tab (see Figure 4-11).

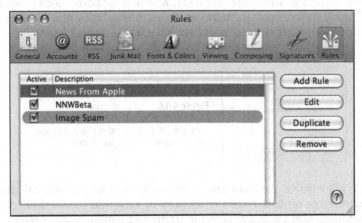

Figure 4-11. Mail's filtering system lets you define rules to apply against your incoming mail messages.

When you receive a new message, Mail executes each of your filters against it by running them in the order they are listed in the filters preferences pane. You can change that order by dragging items up or down the list.

You will notice that a filter's creation process is similar to that of a smart folder. The main difference between a smart folder and a filter is that a smart folder merely aggregates messages from other mailboxes into a transient mailbox, whereas a filter works with the actual messages and is able to move the messages to other folders (among other actions).

You can create a filter that checks almost any condition that an e-mail may have whether it be a standard attribute like a sender, subject text, or message contents, or something more obscure like a MIME type or some other Mail header.

Besides just moving messages between folders using filters, you can also have Mail change the color of a message, play a sound, automatically reply, or execute a script.

One of the areas I have found Mail's filtering most beneficial is when dealing with tech support e-mails. Whenever a message is sent to my company's support e-mail address, I have a message filter set up that will automatically reply with a message letting the user know I have successfully received the message and will be looking into her issue within the next 24 hours.

A great web site dedicated to working more effectively with Mail is Tim Gaden's Hawk Wings. You can visit it at www.hawkwings.net.

Composing e-mail

One of the great things about Mail is that it is easy to use for a novice user, but powerful enough to keep power users satisfied. By default, the new Mail window contains the standard To, CC, Subject, and message text fields. Mail also supports sending blind carbon copies and using custom reply-to addresses. To customize Mail's new message window, click the button to the left of the Subject field and select Customize (see Figure 4-12).

Figure 4-12.
Mail's compose window gives you the bare essentials to send e-mails, but you can customize it to your liking.

The window will animate and show you all the available fields that you can use to customize your message window. Place a check mark by each field you want to add. Besides the recipient fields, Mail also has options for determining what account to send a message from, which SMTP server, what priority to set for a user, and whether to encrypt or digitally sign a message.

Once you have customized your window to your liking, click the OK button to save your changes.

Address book integration

In Mac OS X 10.2 Jaguar, Apple included support for a systemwide contact repository by providing a developer API for working with the Address Book application. This eliminated the need to keep your contacts in multiple locations; instead you can store everything in the system's repository and allow third-party developers to hook into that database.

One application that has made use of that systemwide repository since the beginning of Mac OS X is Mail. There are two ways to work with the system address book in Mail.

The first is by typing addresses in the To, CC, and BCC fields. Mail will automatically try to complete the address by querying your address book and the previous recipients database. Anytime you send a message to someone, that person's e-mail address is automatically appended to the previous recipients database so that you can easily reference that address in future e-mails (see Figure 4-13).

Figure 4-13. Mail supports autocompletion of addresses as you type. It queries your address book and the previous recipients list.

> *You can trim your previous recipients list by going to the* Window *menu and selecting* Previous Recipients.

The second way to work with the address book is by clicking the Address button in the new message toolbar. Clicking the button will open a panel that has a listing of all the contacts in your Address Book (see Figure 4-14). Once you select a message, you can then click one of the buttons at the top that correspond with the field you want that e-mail address to appear in.

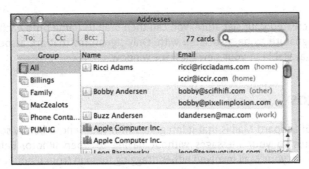

Figure 4-14. The Addresses panel queries your Address Book database.

Signatures

Mail has support for per-account signatures. **Signatures** are just ways to end your e-mail. A signature can be just your name, or can contain something more detailed such as a privacy notice if you are sending corporate mail. For each e-mail account that you have set up in Mail, you can associate one or more signatures with that account. You can then choose to append one of the signatures to the bottom of your e-mail.

Mail manages all of your signatures in its preferences pane. The signatures pane has three vertical columns with your accounts listed on the left, each of your signatures in the middle, and the contents of the currently selected signature on the right.

To create a signature, click the plus (+) button below the middle column and name it (see Figure 4-15). You can then customize it with text, images, or other types of files. You can also further customize your signatures by modifying the fonts: just highlight the text you want to manipulate and select Cmd+T (⌘+T).

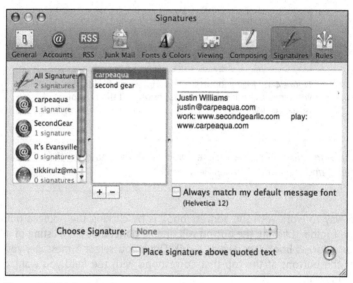

Figure 4-15. Mail supports per-account signatures.

Once you have created your signature, you can then drag its name onto each account that you want the signature to be associated with. Only signatures that are associated with an account will be available in your new message window.

Adding photos

A new feature of Leopard Mail is that it integrates with your iPhoto library so that you can easily add photos to your messages without having to open iPhoto. Before Leopard, adding messages to your Mail involved either dragging them in from iPhoto or creating the e-mail message from within iPhoto. Apple realized that it made sense to include support for the iPhoto library directly from Mail.

To work with photos in Mail, click the Photo Browser button in the new message window and a Photo Browser panel will open with a listing of all your iPhoto photos and albums that you can work with.

To add a photo to a mail message, double-click the photo you want to insert. It will automatically be appended to your message where your cursor is located (see Figure 4-16).

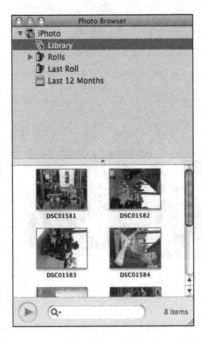

4

Figure 4-16.
Leopard adds support for working with your iPhoto library directly from Mail.

Stationery

One of the biggest features touted in Leopard Mail is the addition of stationery. **Stationery** allows you to send e-mails that have a unique layout, colors, and fonts.

Apple bundles 30 templates by default that have several different styles to choose from. Some of the templates included are for birthday cards, postcards, and get well wishes. Each stationery template is built using standard HTML and CSS so that it will render perfectly not only on other Macs using Mail, but also on a PC user's machine running a mail application such as Microsoft Outlook.

To convert your message to stationery, click the Show Stationery button in the new message toolbar. The Stationery Browser will then appear in the message window. Stationery is separated into four categories: simple, photos, greetings, and invitation. You can easily switch between different stationery templates by clicking each one. Each time you click, your message's styling is transformed to that of the new template (see Figure 4-17).

Figure 4-17. Mail's stationery feature lets you send beautiful e-mails with minimal effort.

If the template you choose has an image included, you can add your own by dragging it in place of the existing image. Mail will automatically resize the photo to fit.

You can even create your own HTML e-mail. After creating a message and styling it as you see fit, go to the File menu and select Save As Stationery. Any stationery that you create will be stored in the Custom section of the Stationery Browser.

Creating tasks

Some mail users, myself included, e-mail themselves reminders of things they need to do in the future. While Apple could allow users to create several notes to keep track of those to-do items, Apple decided it would be better to include new functionality for managing tasks as well. Tasks differ from notes in that you can assign them a due date and priority, and associate them with a calendar in iCal.

Creating a to-do item is simple. Just click the To Do button in the toolbar to switch to the To Do view (see Figure 4-18).

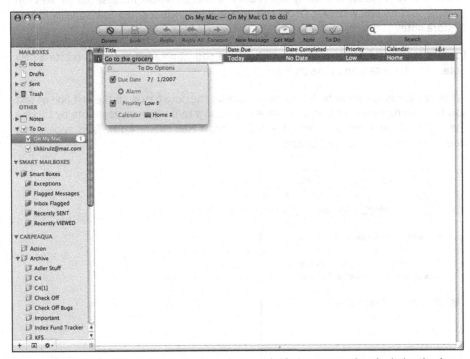

Figure 4-18. To-do items in Mail make it easy to keep track of what you need to do during the day.

When you create a to-do item in Mail, it will add the item to a To Do mailbox in Mail. From there you can modify the title of the task and its priority, and then show it in iCal. To expose the editing view, Control-click the task and select Edit Task.

The tasks stored in Mail are also stored in iCal automatically. No matter which application you edit the data in, the changes will be synced between each application.

Like mail messages, you can store your to-do items on the server if you are connecting to your e-mail account via IMAP. To enable this, follow these steps:

1. Go to Mail's preferences window.

2. Select the Accounts tab.

3. Select the account you want to modify.

4. Go to the Mailbox Behaviors **tab and check** Store To Do information on the server.

Creating notes

Users tend to keep a lot of their life in their inboxes: important items in relation to their job, letters from friends and family, directions to a friend's house. Because our inboxes can become so cluttered, with Mac OS X Leopard Apple has included new functionality in Mail to store notes.

Located in your sidebar is a mailbox with a legal pad icon called Notes. To create a new note, click the Note icon in the toolbar.

When you create a new note, it automatically titles the note based on the first line of text you type. Along with your text, you can also append a to-do item to your note by clicking the To Do button in the toolbar of the note window (see Figure 4-19). Tasks appear in a note with a thick orange background.

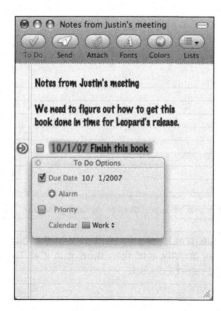

Figure 4-19.
Mail's notes let you add reminders, shopping lists, and other kinds of personal data to your inbox.

A Mail note can contain not only text, but also files and images. If your friend e-mails you directions to his house, you can take those directions and create a note from them and attach a map that may be beneficial when you actually begin driving.

Each Mail account has the option of storing notes in your inbox along with your Mail messages. Notes appear just like any other Mail message. To enable this, follow these steps:

1. Go to Mail's preferences window.

2. Select the Accounts tab.

3. Select the account you want to modify.

4. Go to the Mailbox Behaviors tab and check Store notes in Inbox.

Adding RSS feeds

In Mac OS X Tiger Apple bundled RSS support in Safari, allowing you to either subscribe to an RSS feed from within the browser or pass the feed on to a third-party aggregator like NetNewsWire. In the time since Tiger's release, other mail clients such as Mozilla's Thunderbird have added support for subscribing to RSS feeds. Apple wanted to match this feature and hence added support for RSS into Mail.

Apple extends the Thunderbird model for RSS in Mail by allowing users to import their Safari RSS feeds. To add feeds go to File ➤ Add RSS Feeds. A sheet will pop up that lists your RSS feeds that are stored in Safari. You can easily select those to be added to Mail. If you want to add a feed not included in Safari, you can type its address into the Feed URL text field (see Figure 4-20).

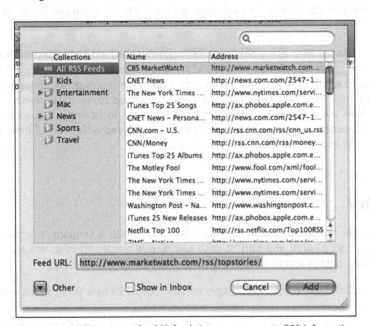

Figure 4-20. Mail's support for RSS feeds lets you aggregate RSS information from any of the feeds stored in your Safari bookmarks.

One option you have is whether or not to include your RSS items in your inbox as well as your notes and mail messages. If you subscribe to several feeds, your inbox may become even more unruly, so you may need to be wary of this feature.

Figure 4-21 shows what a typical RSS item looks like in Mac OS X Leopard.

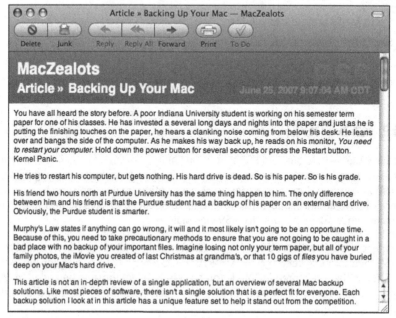

Figure 4-21. RSS items have a blue banner at the top with the feed name, article title, and date.

I don't use Safari or Mail as my dominant RSS aggregator as I am a longtime NetNewsWire user, but one of the workflows I have found works best for Mail's support for RSS feeds is subscribing to my local newspaper. When I wake up in the morning, the first thing I do is check my e-mail. With Mac OS X Leopard, I also subscribed to my local newspaper's RSS feed and have the day's news items included in my inbox so I can get a quick update of what has happened in the past 24 hours. It's only a single feed with 10 to 15 items per day that I can scan and read more of if I'm interested.

Summary

In this chapter, I covered how to work with Mail in Mac OS X Leopard. You saw how to create an e-mail account and how to send and receive e-mails from it. You also learned how to attach photos and use stationery while sending new mail messages.

You also explored more advanced usages of Mail: Leopard's new to-do items, notes, and RSS features.

In the next chapter, I'll cover Safari and iChat, Apple's bundled web browser and chat client.

5 SAFARI AND iCHAT

User Backdrop 4

In this chapter, I will cover the following topics:

- What is Safari
- Bookmarks
- Tabbed browsing
- RSS support
- Private browsing
- What is iChat
- Supported protocols
- Audio and video chatting
- Desktop sharing
- Tabbed chatting
- Multiple protocols

Safari

When Mac OS X was first released in 2001, the only web browser available at that time for the operating system was Microsoft Internet Explorer. Microsoft had done a good job at porting their OS 9 browser to the new OS, but Apple realized that it was showing its age. It had a dated user interface, no tabbed browsing or pop-up blocking, and was behind in terms of web standards support.

The general consensus on the Web is that it is incredibly difficult to make money selling a browser because of the precedent set by Netscape and Microsoft in the late 1990s of giving away the browser for free. It seemed only logical for Apple to develop a browser internally that would complement Mac OS X. Thus, Safari was born.

> *As OS X matured, another browser had emerged: Chimera (now known as Camino), which was built on top of the Mozilla Gecko rendering engine. In fact, one of the main developers of the Camino project was David Hyatt, who Apple hired to lead the Safari team.*
>
> *Camino is still developed today and available at* http://caminobrowser.org.

Using Safari

Using Safari is easy. When you first launch your Mac, you will see Safari's compass icon in your Dock. If you don't see it, you can quickly open the application from the Applications folder. At the top of the Safari window are navigation buttons to jump between web pages (see Figure 5-1). The left and right arrows let you navigate between web pages you visited during your current browsing session. Next to these buttons is the Refresh button, which will reload the page you are currently visiting.

Figure 5-1. Safari is the default web browser bundled with Mac OS X.

New to Leopard is the Web Clip button. **Web Clip** let you turn a part of any web page into a Dashboard widget. I'll cover Web Clip in depth in Chapter 6. The plus (+) button lets you add the page you are currently viewing to your bookmarks.

The long bar with the globe is the **address bar**. This is where you enter the web site's address, or URL, you want to visit. On the far-right end of the Safari toolbar is the Google search bar. When you type something into that field and press the Return key, it will search for the text you typed via Google.

To visit a web page via Safari, just type the URL into the address bar and press the Return key. The page will render in Safari's main viewing area. You can watch the progress of your page rendering by following the blue bar that appears in the address bar. As it moves closer to the right edge, more of your page will be viewable.

Snapback

One of my favorite features of Safari is Snapback. As you are looking for things via Google, you can drift far away from your initial search results page. With Snapback, you can easily jump back to your initial results without having to repeatedly hit the Back button.

Snapback appears as an orange arrow icon in the Google search bar (see Figure 5-2). Clicking it will take you directly back to your search results page.

Figure 5-2. Snapback makes it easy to quickly go back to your search results no matter how many pages you have visited since the search.

Bookmarks

One of the major features touted when Safari was first released was its new take on managing bookmarks. Prior to Safari, bookmarks were handled in a linear fashion via a menu by all browsers. Apple realized that as you begin to amass a collection of bookmarks, it can be somewhat unruly to manage those bookmarks.

Apple decided it would be better to have a bookmark management solution built into the browser.

To access the bookmarks manager, go to the Bookmarks menu and select Show All Bookmarks.

The bookmarks manager puts the bookmark folders in a source list on the left and a listing of actual bookmarks on the right (see Figure 5-3).

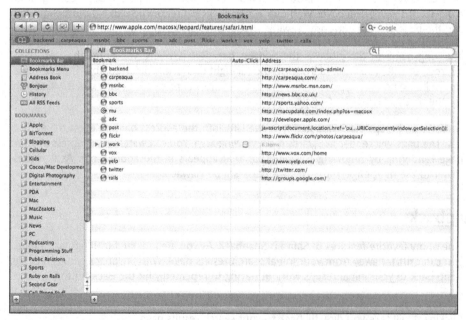

Figure 5-3. Safari's bookmarks manager makes it easy to sort and search through your bookmarks.

Besides the folders that you manually create, Safari also has a set of standard collections:

- **Bookmarks Bar:** The bookmarks that show up just below the address bar.
- **Bookmarks Menu:** The listing of bookmarks that appear in the Bookmarks menu item in the Safari menu bar.
- **Address Book:** All URLs included in your address book contacts.
- **Bonjour:** If you have other Macs on your local network with web-sharing enabled, they are discoverable using Apple's Bonjour technology.
- **History:** Your browsing history.
- **All RSS Feeds:** Any RSS feed that you have saved in your bookmarks.

You can also search all of your bookmarks using the integrated search field in the bookmarks manager.

Tabbed browsing

One of the major trends in web browsing in the past five years is the introduction of tabbed browsing. **Tabbed browsing** allows you to open multiple web pages all in a single browser window. To access each page you have open, you click the tab in your toolbar (see Figure 5-4).

Figure 5-4. Tabbed browsing lets you visit multiple web sites in the same browser window, thus reducing desktop clutter.

With the introduction of Mac OS X Leopard, Apple has enabled tabbed browsing by default. To open a browser in a new tab, go to File ➤ New Tab. The Safari tab bar will then appear under your bookmarks bar.

The tab bar has an X in a circle on the far left that closes each tab. Each tab also has the title of the web page associated with that tab. You can rearrange your tabs by dragging them either left or right in the tab bar. This is also another new feature of Leopard that makes Safari's tab management even easier. Want to have a tab displayed in its own window? Just drag it out of the tab bar like you would an icon in the Dock. The page will expand into its own window.

Private browsing

There are times when you are surfing the Web that you won't want Safari to keep track of your tracks. If you are in a public location such as library, you can enable Safari's private browsing feature, which causes the browser to not keep track of the sites you visit, nor will it cache the data or create cookies from the site. To enable private browsing, click Private

Browsing in the Safari menu (see Figure 5-5). A confirmation dialog box will appear with an explanation of what the feature does.

Figure 5-5. Private browsing lets you surf without keeping track of your history.

Web Clip

One of the major new features of Dashboard in Mac OS X Leopard is the Web Clip feature. Web Clip allows you to turn any portion of a web page into a Dashboard widget. I will cover this feature, and Mac OS X's Dashboard feature, in depth in Chapter 6.

RSS support

The major feature of Safari in Mac OS X Tiger was its inclusion of RSS support. RSS is a technology for content distribution. RSS allows site publishers to easily distribute their information to readers; likewise, it allows readers to pull content from any site that supports RSS without having to visit the actual site.

RSS files consist of standard XML marked up in a format that browsers like Safari can understand.

Using your web browser, you could detect and read RSS feeds (or pass them to a third-party RSS feed reader of your choice). When you go to a web site that has an RSS feed, such as http://maczealots.com/, an RSS icon will appear in the far-right corner of your browser's address bar as in Figure 5-6.

Figure 5-6. If a site has an RSS feed embedded in it, the blue RSS button will appear at the far-right end of the address bar.

Clicking the icon will transform Safari's browser window into its RSS view, which transforms the RSS feed's information into a readable format, as shown in Figure 5-7.

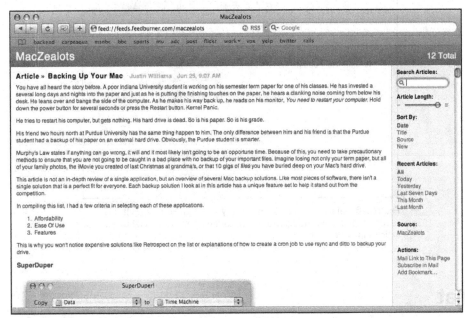

Figure 5-7. Safari's RSS view lets you easily see the content of a web page without all the style surrounding it.

Once you find an RSS feed for a site you are interested in, you can save it with your bookmarks so you can reference it later. You can then reference it like any other bookmark you may have stored.

What makes RSS feeds so great though is that RSS feeds are automatically updated (every 30 minutes by default). You can have Safari highlight the new items.

1. Go to Safari ➤ Preferences.

2. Click the RSS button.

3. Make sure that the option Color new articles is checked (see Figure 5-8).

If you find that Safari's RSS support is not everything you want, you can have Safari pass off RSS feeds to a third-party aggregator like NetNewsWire. To do this, follow these steps:

1. Go to Safari ➤ Preferences.

2. Click the RSS button.

3. Change the Default RSS Reader setting to your preferred reader (see Figure 5-8).

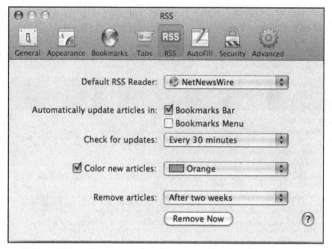

Figure 5-8. Safari's RSS preferences let you assign your default RSS reader, specify your update time, and define how to highlight new articles in your feeds.

iChat

iChat is Mac OS X's bundled instant messaging client (see Figure 5-9). iChat primarily supports the popular AOL Instant Messenger (AIM) protocol, but also has embedded support for Bonjour and Jabber messaging. Bonjour, Apple's network technology, easily finds other computers connected to your local network with no configuration. Jabber is an open instant messaging protocol used by many different services, including Google Talk.

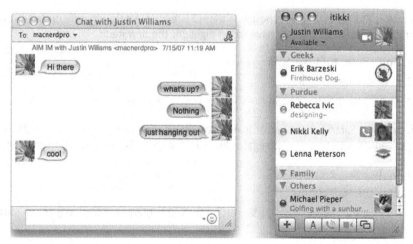

Figure 5-9. iChat in Leopard adds improved support for buddy groups, but still keeps the goofy chat bubble for IM messages.

Besides text-based chats, iChat also has embedded support for audio and video chats. iChat's AV support can interface not only with other iChat users, but also Windows users who are using the latest versions of the instant messenger client.

Tabbed chats

Like tabbed browsing in Safari, Apple supports grouping multiple IM conversations into a single window in iChat. iChat takes a different approach to tabs by putting the tabs on the left side of the window rather than under the title bar, as shown in Figure 5-10.

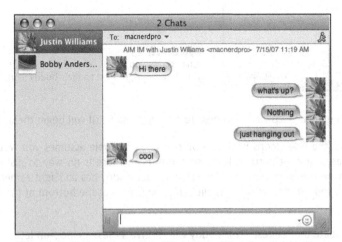

Figure 5-10. Tabbed chats work differently in iChat than they do in other applications like Safari in that the tabs appear vertically on the side rather than horizontally below the title bar.

Tabbed chatting is turned off by default, but you can enable it easily:

1. Go to iChat ➤ Preferences.

2. Click the Messages button.

3. Make sure that the option Collect chats into a single window is checked.

Audio and video chats

Besides just text chats, iChat excels at also doing multimedia chats via audio or video. In the past few years, Apple has included both a microphone and a video camera in their portable machines and their iMac line. This makes it easy to have an audio or a video conference wherever you are without the need to carry around extra peripherals.

Creating an audio chat

Having an audio chat in iChat is as easy as a button click. If you look at your Buddy List window, you will see a green telephone or video camera icon next to anyone who is capable of having an audio or a video chat (see Figure 5-11).

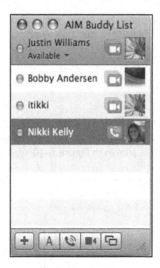

Figure 5-11.
iChat shows you the audio and video status of
your buddies right next to their buddy icons.

If you click the green telephone icon next to a buddy's name, it will begin the audio chat.

In the case of the video icons next to a person's name, Apple assumes you would like to not only hear your chat partner, but also see him, so there is no way to just initiate an audio chat from the green buddy list icons when your buddy has an iSight camera enabled as well. What you can do, however, is click the phone icon at the bottom of the Buddy List window.

When you initiate the request, your buddy will receive a message pop-up letting her know that you would like to chat with her. If she accepts, the audio chat connection will begin (see Figure 5-12).

Figure 5-12. Audio chats let you explain things
to your buddies when text just won't do.

iChat supports audio conferences with up to ten different buddies, so you can eliminate the need for the conference room speaker phones. To add another user to your iChat audio chat, just click the + button and select a name from the list of available buddies. The chat window will morph to show the volume level of each contact as well as his name and buddy icon.

Creating a video chat

Nobody does video conferencing as well as Apple does with its combination of iSight and iChat software. While the general functionality is the same in Leopard as it was in Tiger, Apple has added some neat features such as iPhoto integration and custom backdrops to liven up your iChat experience even more.

To start a video chat, find a buddy on your buddy list with the camera icon next to his name and click it. A window will pop up with a preview of what your buddy will see when the video chat goes active. This is your time to primp your hair and adjust your camera accordingly (see Figure 5-13).

Figure 5-13. When waiting for a video conference, you can adjust your camera's view to be perfect so that your buddy can see all of you when the chat begins.

Once the user on the other end accepts the invitation, your camera will shrink to a smaller box in the corner, and the window will be filled with the contents of your buddy's camera, as shown in Figure 5-14.

Figure 5-14. iChat has a picture-in-picture view so that you can see your camera as well as your buddy's during a chat.

At the bottom of the video chat window are four buttons. The Effects button lets you use Photo Booth effects to distort your image. The + button lets you add a third person to your chat. The middle button lets you mute your microphone, and the button with the arrows on it allows you to make the chat window full screen.

Applying Photo Booth effects

While I won't be covering Photo Booth in depth until Chapter 16, it is beneficial to show you how to apply Photo Booth effects to your iChat video chats. Photo Booth effects let you distort your video in fun ways. You can give yourself a neon outline or mirror your image to look like you are in a carnival attraction.

To work with the effects, go to the Video menu in iChat and select Show Video Effects. A HUD will appear with a sample of what each effect looks like with the video feed from your iSight camera (see Figure 5-15).

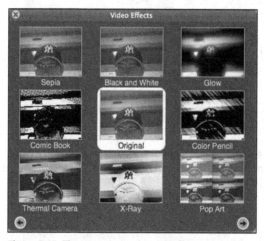

Figure 5-15. There are more than 20 effects to annoy your friends with when having an iChat video chat.

Clicking an effect will automatically apply that effect to the video being sent to your friend's Mac (see Figure 5-16). To change your filter, just click another one from the Composition Picker.

To erase a video effect, click the Original tab in the middle of the video effects HUD. This will revert your image back to its normal state.

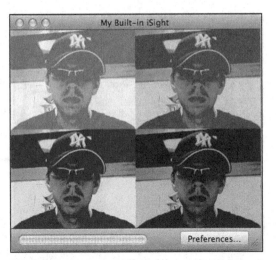

Figure 5-16. The pop-art effect makes your camera's video look like a set of Andy Warhol silkscreens.

Changing the background

One of the main features of iChat's improved video chat support in Leopard is the ability to change the background of your chat with a picture or movie. If you are a golfer, you can have the background of your video chats be a photo of your favorite golf course, or you can set the video to be of a waterfall near the eighteenth green.

You can set the background of your video chat in the same place as you add video effects—the video effects HUD. At the bottom of the HUD are two arrow icons that let you browse all the effects (see Figure 5-17). Click one of the arrow icons to page through the effects and backgrounds.

Figure 5-17. The video effects HUD has arrow keys that let you browse all the effects and custom backgrounds available to you.

When you find a background you are satisfied with, click it and then step out of the frame of your camera. You need to exit the frame so that iChat can detect the background. When it is ready, the screen will notify you that you can step back into frame, and the background will mix with your figure (see Figure 5-18).

Figure 5-18. iChat includes backgrounds such as Times Square, Yosemite National Park, and a roller coaster.

iChat also has support for custom iChat backgrounds of your own. For example, if you have a beautiful photo from your trip to Italy, you can add it to the effects HUD. To do this, follow these steps:

1. Open the video effects HUD and scroll to page 5/5 where there are several options for user backdrops.

2. Find a photo on your Mac that you want to use as a backdrop and drag it onto one of the User Backdrop wells (see Figure 5-19).

Figure 5-19. User backdrops let you use your own photos as the background of your iChat video chats.

Like video effects, to erase a custom backdrop, click the Original tab in the middle of the video effects HUD. This will revert your image back to its normal state.

iChat Theater

One of my favorite features in iChat is the new Theater feature. Many times I want to show a file or PDF document to a coworker throughout the day. Previously, I'd have to send it via e-mail and wait for the user to open it. Now, I can talk the user through changes in the document via iChat video conferences. To use iChat Theater, do the following:

1. Initiate a video conference with another user.

2. Go to the Video menu and select Share With iChat Theater.

3. In the dialog that pops up, select the file you want to share. You can share PDFs, Word and text documents, Excel documents, and Keynote presentations. iChat Theater works with any file type that works with Quick Look (see Figure 5-20).

Figure 5-20. With iChat Theater, you can share PDFs and presentations with other iChat users.

If you want to share a set of photos, you can do that as well. Just select the group of photos in step 3, and then iChat will navigate through them as a slideshow for both you and your video partner while you act as the narrator.

Desktop sharing

Another new feature introduced in Mac OS X Leopard's version of iChat is support for sharing your desktop with another user over iChat. This feature is useful if you want to show a friend in another office or across the globe something on your Mac. This is a feature that has been available for Mac OS X for a while as a part of Apple's Remote Desktop application, but is aimed more at system administrators rather than consumers.

One of the greatest benefits of built-in screen sharing is that it will make your job as the computer geek of the family much easier. The next time grandma has trouble getting her e-mail, rather than having to drive to her house, you can merely initiate a screen-sharing session via iChat and fix the problem for her right there.

Sharing your screen

To initiate screen sharing, both users need to be running Mac OS X Leopard. In your iChat buddy window, select the user you want to initiate the sharing session with and then click the new Screen Sharing button at the bottom of the Buddy List window. It looks like two squares overlapping each other (see Figure 5-21).

Figure 5-21. Mac OS X Leopard gives you the option of sharing your screen or a remote user's screen.

A menu pops up giving you the option to share your screen or to view the other person's screen. Clicking Share My Screen will pop up a window that lets you know the user has been pinged with a request to share your screen (see Figure 5-22).

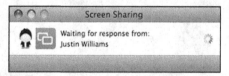

Figure 5-22. On your machine, you will see a screen like this letting you know that your request for screen sharing has been sent to the receiving party.

On the other end of the connection, the person you want to share your screen with will see a semitranslucent black window with your buddy icon and name like in Figure 5-23.

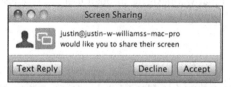

Figure 5-23. On the receiving end of the request, the other party will see a screen like this letting that user know you want to initiate a screen-sharing session.

If the user accepts your request to share his screen, your screen will be overtaken by what he sees, and your desktop will appear in the bottom of the Window much as if your video were in an iChat video conference (see Figure 5-24).

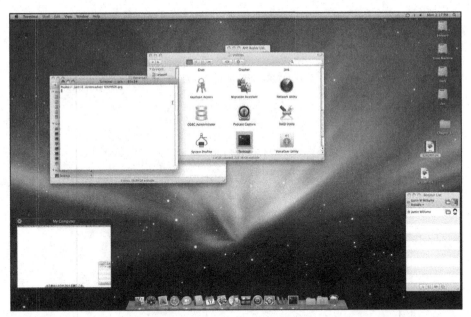

Figure 5-24. When the other party accepts your invitation, your volume options are enabled.

When you are done sharing screens, you can click the X on the pager in the lower-left corner to end the sharing session.

Viewing a remote screen

In the instance of seeing your grandmother's screen I talked about earlier, you will want to share her screen rather than your own. To do this, click the Screen Sharing button at the bottom of the Buddy List window and this time select Share Buddy's Screen where *Buddy* is the name of the person.

If the other party accepts, your screen will appear in the pager in the lower-left corner, and what she sees will become your main screen. The functionality is the same as working with your screen, but the roles are reversed.

Multiple sign-ins

One of the points of contention many power users have had against iChat is its lack of support for logging on to multiple accounts at the same time. With Mac OS X Leopard, Apple now supports multiple sign-ins, though not in a way you might assume.

If you have two AIM accounts you would like to have signed in, iChat creates a separate buddy list for each account rather than consolidating your buddies all in a single list like clients such as Adium or Windows's Trillian do.

To enable multiple accounts, go to the Accounts preference pane in iChat's preference and add each account you want to enable to your account listing. Make sure that each account you want logged in has Use this account checked, as shown in Figure 5-25.

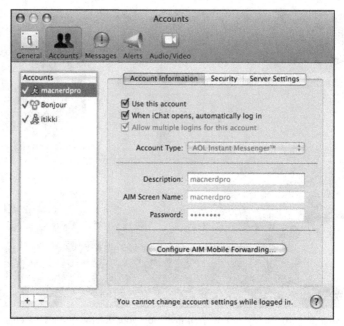

Figure 5-25. The iChat account management window is located in iChat's preferences.

If you want to log out of one of your accounts, the process is somewhat unintuitive. Make the buddy list for the account you want to log out of the frontmost window and then go to your iChat menu and select Logout of *account* (where *account* is your AIM screen name), as shown in Figure 5-26.

Figure 5-26. To log out of an account, go to the iChat menu and select the Log Out menu item.

Summary

In this chapter, I covered two of the biggest applications in Mac OS X Leopard: Safari and iChat. You saw how to use Safari as your web browser, read RSS feeds with it, and better organize your browsing session with tabbed browsing.

You also learned about using iChat for text, audio, and video chats. I introduced the new iChat Theater feature and screen sharing.

In the next chapter, I'll introduce the Mac OS X Dashboard—Apple's awesome widget platform.

5

6 DASHBOARD

This chapter covers the following topics:

- What is Dashboard
- Adding and removing widgets
- Finding new widgets
- Managing your widgets
- Web clips

One of the main selling points of the previous version of Mac OS X, 10.4 Tiger, was Dashboard. Dashboard allows users to run mini-applications called **widgets** that perform small, common tasks easily. Whether you want to quickly get access to the current temperature or look up a phone number in the yellow pages, a Dashboard widget makes it only a mouse click away.

One of the major complaints about Dashboard in Mac OS X Tiger was that each Dashboard widget was contained in its own instance of the Dashboard client. With Leopard, Apple rearchitectured how Dashboard widgets are run on your system so that only one instance of your Dashboard client application is running. Each widget is stored in that single client, which helps reduce Dashboard's memory footprint as you open more and more widgets.

Besides the smaller memory footprint, Dashboard is up to also two times faster in Leopard than it was in Mac OS X Tiger. You can notice this in several areas. For one, there is no longer the initial delay for your widgets to pull data in when you launch Dashboard for the first time. The process is now almost instantaneous.

When you launch Mac OS X, a black compass icon sits in your Dock to the left of the Address Book icon (see Figure 6-1). Clicking it puts a mildly translucent overlay on your system as well as your currently visible widgets so you can work with them while the rest of your Mac waits for you in the background.

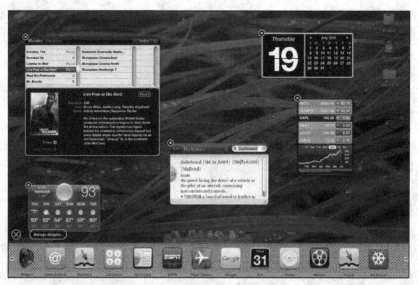

Figure 6-1. Dashboard widgets make performing small tasks like checking stocks and getting the current date easy.

Working with widgets

Dashboard's incredibly easy to work with. Apple bundles 20 widgets that you can use on your Dashboard. To start using these widgets, click the Dashboard icon in your Dock to bring up Dashboard.

In the bottom-left corner of the window, you will see a plus sign in a circle, as shown in Figure 6-2. Clicking this will bring up the widget browser. The **widget browser** is a bar that runs along the bottom of your screen and displays the icons for each of the widgets installed on your system.

Figure 6-2.
Clicking the plus icon will bring up the widget browser.

The bar shows thirteen widgets at a time. You can page through all of your widgets by moving your mouse to the left or right side of the browser bar and clicking the arrow button.

To add a new widget to your Dashboard, just click the widget's icon and it will appear in your Dashboard with a very impressive water ripple effect behind it. The widget appears in the middle of your screen, but you can use your mouse to move it wherever you want on your screen.

Removing widgets from your Dashboard is just as easy. With the widget manager open, each of your widgets has a black X icon in the upper-left corner. Clicking that icon will remove a widget from your Dashboard. It does not physically remove it from your system. Your widget still remains in the widget manager so you can read it in the future.

> If you want to save a step in removing a widget, hold down the Option key as you hover your mouse pointer over a widget. This will make the black X appear, and you can close the widget.

Finding new widgets

While Apple bundles several useful widgets with Mac OS X Leopard, there are thousands of widgets available on the Web to further enhance your Dashboard experience. The best resource for finding these widgets is Apple's own Dashboard widget download page (www.apple.com/downloads/dashboard/). Apple organizes the widgets by category and also provides a search option so you can find other widgets based on your preferences (see Figure 6-3). Besides the widget listings, Apple also offers Staff Picks and a listing of the Top 50 widgets based on downloads by other Mac users around the world.

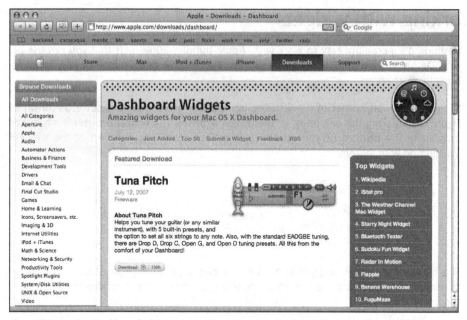

Figure 6-3. Apple's Dashboard gives you a fairly comprehensive list of the widgets created for Mac OS X.

To use a widget you find on this site, simply click the Download link on the widget. Safari will download the widget to your desktop and ask if you would like to install it (see Figure 6-4).

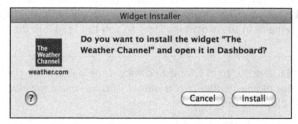

Figure 6-4. Before a widget is installed on your Mac, your Mac asks if you want to install it.

Clicking the Install button will put the widget into Dashboard's testing area. The testing area is used to let you test out a widget before finally committing to installing it on your machine (see Figure 6-5). If you decide not to keep the widget, it will instead be moved to the trash.

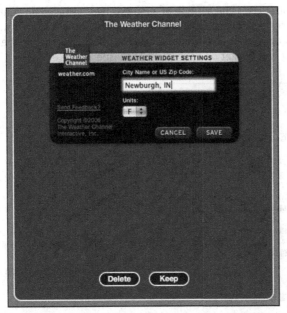

Figure 6-5. Dashboard allows you to test a widget before finally installing it on your Mac. If you don't like a widget, click Delete and it will be put in the trash automatically.

Most widgets are freely available, but there are a few that are shareware and cost a few dollars. Since installing and using widgets is so easy, don't hesitate to experiment with as many widgets as you'd like.

Managing widgets

As you accumulate widgets on your system, your widget manager might become a bit unruly. Apple includes a widget designed to manage your widget collection. Using it, you can disable widgets so that they don't appear in the manager window. They aren't deleted from your system, only hidden from the widget manager.

To open the widget organizer, open the widget manager and click the Widgets icon (see Figure 6-6).

Figure 6-6.
The widget organizer lets you enable and disable certain widgets so they don't appear in the widget manager.

The widget organizer gives you a listing of all the widgets installed on your Mac. To the left of the widget's icon is a check box. If the check box is checked, the widget is enabled. Unchecking a check box beside a widget will remove that widget from the widget manager and any copies of that widget on your Dashboard (see Figure 6-7).

Figure 6-7.
The widget organizer lets you organize your widgets.

> If you want to physically remove a widget from your Mac, go to the Home Folder/Library/Widgets folder and drag the widget you want off your system into the trash.

Web clips

The biggest feature added to Mac OS X Leopard in terms of Dashboard is the introduction of web clips. The **web clips** feature lets you turn any web page into a widget easily. For example, if you wanted a widget to retrieve the schedule for your favorite football team, but couldn't find one that already existed, you could create one using web clips. Want to see your local television station's doppler radar in a widget? Web clips can do that, too.

This feature works by launching an instance of the web page in a widget window resized and positioned to only show the exact portion of the page you want to see. The rest of the page is still available.

Creating a new widget with web clips is an easy process. Just follow these steps.

Figure 6-8.
The Web Clips toolbar icon

1. Launch Safari and go to a web page you are interested in turning into a widget.
2. Click the black Web Clips icon in your Safari toolbar (see Figure 6-8).

3. Once clicked, a purple overlay will slide down from the top of your browser's window, and a portion of your page will be highlighted (see Figure 6-9).

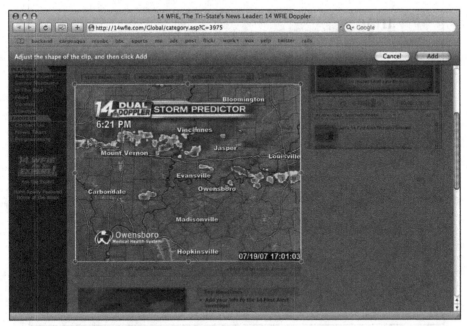

Figure 6-9. The web clips feature lets you highlight the section of a web site you would like to convert into a Dashboard widget.

4. Drag the highlighted area over the portion of the web page you want to be widgetized and resize it accordingly.

5. Once you are satisfied with your selection, click the Add button to add it to your Dashboard.

Once your widget is created, it will be refreshed each time you launch your Dashboard.

Syncing your widgets

Dashboard 2.0 also includes support for synchronizing your widgets between multiple computers with .Mac. If you are a .Mac subscriber, you can enable syncing in the .Mac preferences pane. No longer will you have to install the same widgets locally on both your desktop and portable.

To enable syncing of your widgets, follow these steps

1. Open the System Preferences application.

2. Click the .Mac icon, followed by the Sync tab (see Figure 6-10).

3. Ensure that Dashboard Widgets is checked.

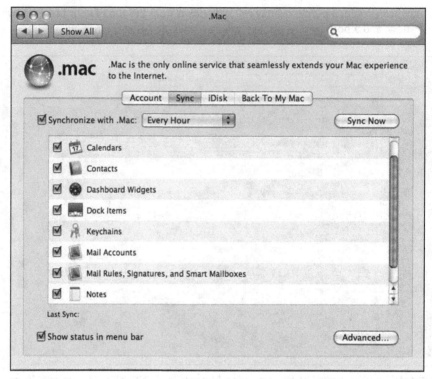

Figure 6-10. You can synchronize your Dashboard widgets between multiple Macs in Mac OS X Leopard with your .Mac account.

Besides syncing the actual widgets on your system, .Mac will also keep track of your widget's preferences and their position on your Dashboard so you can find your widgets in the same location on multiple machines.

Developers don't need to do anything to enable syncing of their Dashboard widgets. It is all configured by Mac OS X, so there shouldn't be any need to update your existing widgets to support .Mac synchronization.

Summary

In this chapter, I covered Mac OS X's Dashboard feature. I introduced you to the Dashboard feature and how to add and remove widgets from it. You also saw how to find new widgets using Apple's online Downloads site. In case you end up with a lot of widgets on your Mac, I covered how to organize your widgets.

You also learned about the new web clips feature, which allows you to turn any portion of a web page into a widget. Finally, I showed you how to synchronize your widgets between multiple Macs using Apple's .Mac service.

The next chapter covers Exposé and Spaces, two features that make it easy to manage having multiple applications and windows open on your Mac.

7 EXPOSÉ AND SPACES

This chapter covers the following topics:

- What is Exposé
- Setting up and using Exposé
- What is Spaces
- Switching between desktops
- Moving applications between desktops
- Binding applications to specific desktops

What is Exposé

One of the biggest problems with having more computing power in your Mac is that you can run multiple applications at once and not really notice too much of a slowdown. You probably have several browser windows, iChat conversations, and a few e-mails open all at the same time during the day. As you keep opening more and more windows on your desktop, others get pushed to the back, and it can sometimes be hard to find that tiny chat window or animated GIF you were working on in Adobe ImageReady.

Apple aimed to solve that problem with Exposé. **Exposé** allows you to quickly see all the windows presently visible on your Mac desktop by pressing F9. Exposé works by scaling all your windows using the Mac OS X's Quartz graphics engine (see Figure 7-1). Once in Exposé mode, you can then highlight over each window with your mouse to get the window's title. Clicking a selected window scales all your windows back to normal size and brings the clicked window to the front.

Figure 7-1. Exposé gives you an overview of all the windows you currently have visible on your Mac.

Besides showing all visible windows, Exposé can also scale only the windows of a single application. For example, if you have several photographs to be edited in Photoshop, you can press the F10 key and have all of those windows scale to a small enough size so that they can all be visible at once.

> *If you are using a MacBook, MacBook Pro, or Powerbook that has a backlit keyboard, you will have to press the function key (fn) in addition to F9 and F10.*

The final mode of Exposé lets you quickly gain access to your Mac's desktop. By pressing the F11 key, all visible windows will quickly slide off to the side of your Macs desktop so that your entire desktop is visible (see Figure 7-2). When you are done working with your desktop, you can press the F11 key once more to have your windows return to where they initially were.

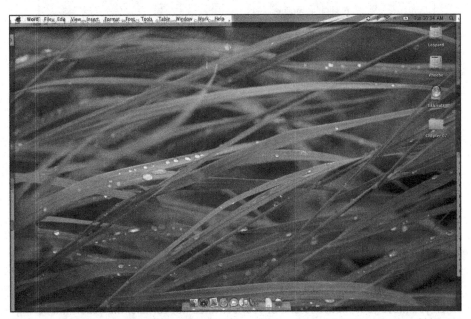

Figure 7-2. The F11 key hides all the visible windows so you can have quick access to your desktop.

Setting up and using Exposé

Besides the standard F9 to F11 keyboard shortcuts already discussed, there are other ways you can configure Exposé to work for you. The place to make all of these changes is in the Exposé & Spaces preferences pane (see Figure 7-3). From there, you can modify the keyboard and mouse shortcuts that are used for each Exposé option as well as set hot corners.

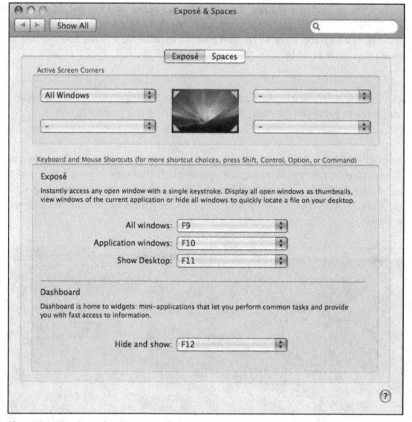

Figure 7-3. The Exposé & Spaces preferences pane is the main hub for setting all options related to Exposé.

Hot corners allow you to drag your mouse to one of the four corners of your Mac's desktop and have OS X trigger an action. Available actions include all three Exposé actions: showing the Dashboard and starting or stopping your screensaver. Each corner is allowed one mapped action.

When you move your mouse to one of your activated hot corners, the action will be triggered instantly.

What is Spaces?

Many studies have been performed that show that having more than one monitor connected to your computer makes you a more productive worker. Unfortunately, adding a second screen to your Mac is an expensive prospect. In some cases, such as if you are using a laptop, it's not even practical. With Leopard, Apple has given you the next best thing: a virtual screen.

As discussed earlier, Exposé makes it easy to sort through the clutter that can become your desktop as you begin working with several applications on your Mac. Spaces aims to refine that organization even more by allowing you to segregate your applications onto several virtual desktops. You can create a screen for your e-mail and iChat conversations, one for your Word documents, and another one to work on the iMovie you are making of your last vacation.

With Spaces, you can create up to 16 virtual desktops to help keep you organized. To get started with that, open up System Preferences and go to the Exposé & Spaces preferences pane.

By default, Apple ships Mac OS X Leopard with Spaces disabled. Apple assumes it is more of a power-user feature and doesn't want to confuse novice users by having them accidentally switching between desktops and thinking they lost all of their applications or documents.

Under the Spaces tab, click the Enable Spaces check box option to turn on the feature (see Figure 7-4). You can also set up a default function key to activate the Spaces view. When you click the key, a snapshot of each of your desktops will overlay your Mac's desktop so you can easily switch between them (similar to how Exposé works).

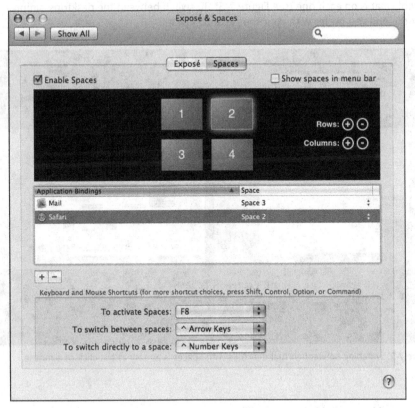

Figure 7-4. The Exposé & Spaces preferences pane allows you to enable Spaces with a single button click.

The Spaces tab allows you to configure all the options associated with the feature. You can configure the number of virtual desktops you want, bind applications to a specific desktop, and set your navigation shortcuts.

Spaces builds a matrix of virtual desktops on your Mac. It then assigns each desktop a specific number starting in the upper-left corner with number 1 and then working its way to the right.

By default, Apple configures Spaces with four virtual desktops. Spaces organizes your virtual desktops using a row and column matrix. To add another desktop, simply click the Add button in the Row or Column section. You'll notice that Spaces automatically adds the correct number of virtual desktops to maintain the matrix integrity. For example, if you have four desktops set up in a 2×2 layout and decide to add a row of desktops, it will add another two desktops to the bottom, giving you a total of six.

Switching between desktops

Once all of your desktops are configured, there are several different ways to navigate through them. The first is by pressing the function key mapped to Spaces. By default, this is F8. Pressing that key will slide all of your desktops onto the screen so you have a central view of what is on each one (see Figure 7-5). To switch between the desktops, simply highlight the one you prefer with your mouse and click it.

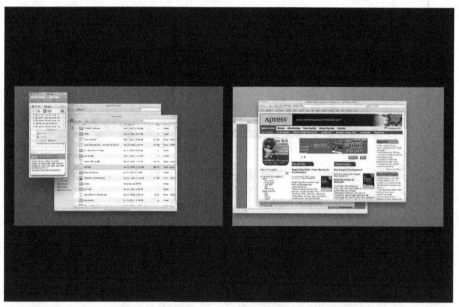

Figure 7-5. Switching between virtual desktops with Spaces is as easy as the click of a mouse.

You can also navigate between desktops using the keyboard. By default, Apple binds Control and the arrow keys to this. In other words, to switch to the desktop to the left of your current one, press Control+left arrow. To move to one above, press Control+up arrow. You can also trigger a specific desktop by number by pressing the Control key and the number of the corresponding desktop.

When you switch between desktops using the key bindings, a small black pager will overlay a portion of your Mac's desktop and show you what desktop you are being switched into and where it is in proximity to the others in your desktop matrix.

You can modify the default keyboard shortcuts to use a different modifier key than the Control key. Your options include the Option key and Cmd key. When you select the pull-down menu (see Figure 7-6), hold down either the Option or Cmd key to append that to your keyboard shortcut.

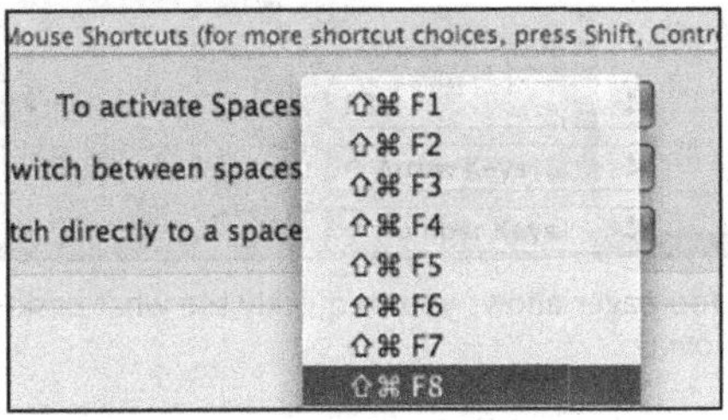

Figure 7-6. You can append modifiers to your keyboard and mouse shorcuts.

You can also choose to disable the navigation shortcuts altogether if you find that they are interfering with one of your applications by selecting the – (dash) option at the bottom of the pull-down menu.

If you want to navigate between your virtual desktops using your mouse, check the Show spaces in menu bar *check box option in the* Exposé & Spaces *preferences pane.*

Moving applications between desktops

Spaces allows you to move your applications between different virtual desktops as you are working with them. There are two ways to do this. The first is to drag the application to the side of the desktop you want to move to and wait for Spaces to swap desktops. As it switches between desktops, the desktop pager will appear on your screen highlighting the desktop that is being switched to and the direction that the movement is taking (see Figure 7-7).

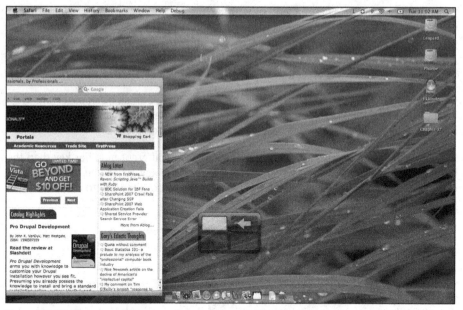

Figure 7-7. The Spaces desktop pager allows you to quickly see what desktop you are presently at and the direction you are moving.

The other way to move applications between desktops is by pressing your Spaces function key to show the Spaces navigator. Once there, you can click and hold down on one of the visible windows and drag it to the desktop of your choice. Once you have the window over your preferred desktop, release your mouse button, and the window will now reside there.

> *You can also click and drag an entire desktop to move it around in your desktop matrix.*

Binding applications to specific desktops

The final feature of Spaces is that you can bind an application to a specific desktop in your matrix. For example, a Mac software developer may want to bind Xcode to a specific desktop and Interface Builder to the adjacent one. Each time those applications are then launched, they will be opened up on their respective desktops according to the binding rule.

To set up an application binding, click the plus (+) button in the Exposé & Spaces preferences pane (see Figure 7-8). In the pane that drops down, browse to your specific application and select it. After selecting your application, you can then select what virtual desktop you want your application to open in every time. You can also set an application to open in any space. By default, an application will open in your currently selected space.

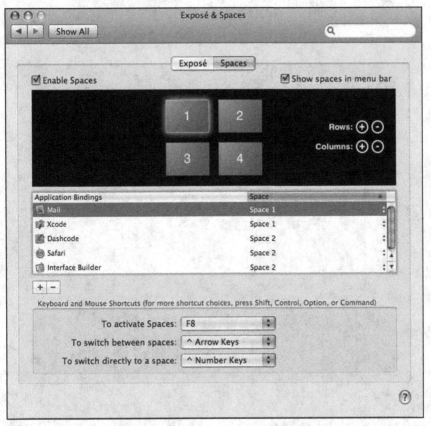

Figure 7-8. You can bind specific applications to a specific Spaces desktop or set it to be visible on any desktop.

When you open an application that has a binding set up, you will automatically be shifted to the desktop that it is bound to. To disable this functionality, go back to the Exposé & Spaces preferences pane and select the application you'd like to remove and click the minus (–) button.

Summary

In this chapter, I covered two productive features built into Mac OS X Leopard: Exposé and Spaces. You learned what Exposé is and how to use it to help manage desktop clutter. You also explored the new Spaces feature in Mac OS X Leopard, which allows you to set up multiple virtual desktops.

Features like these are what differentiate the Mac OS X experience from Windows Vista. In the next chapter, we'll cover another feature that helps separate the two systems: Time Machine.

8 TIME MACHINE

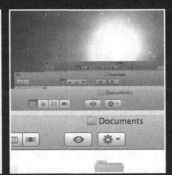

This chapter covers the following topics:

- What is Time Machine
- How Time Machine works
- Configuring Time Machine
- Restoring files

You back up your Mac regularly, right? Be honest. The truth is that most people don't back up their Mac because it's not something they think about until the worst of times: when they have lost their data. There is a good chance that at some point in your computer-using career, you are going to lose data that is important to you from hardware failure such as a hard-disk crash. If your disk crashes and you don't have a backup, all of those family photos, school assignments, or home movies may be lost forever.

What about just common user error? One moment you decide you want to delete a Keynote presentation that you no longer need, but you find out a few days later that your boss wants a copy of it. What are you going to do without a backup?

If the odds are against us in terms of being safe from data loss, why do we avoid backing up our computers? Apple thinks that it is because the process has never been easy. Usually, the process involves getting a secondary hard drive like a FireWire drive and installing it. Once you have done that, you could go through the process of manually copying files to the drive periodically or try to automate the process with third-party software.

Neither option is completely ideal. In the case of the former, you have to remember to copy the files to your drive frequently so that you have the latest versions of your files. In the case of the latter, most third-party solutions are not easy to use. Apple decided to address the issue and build seamless backups into Mac OS X Leopard. This new feature is called **Time Machine**.

How Time Machine backs up your data

Time Machine works in the background, so that once you set it up, you don't have to think about it again until you need it. Time Machine launches a daemon called **backupd** that performs all the backup tasks. Since it's a daemon, it's completely transparent to the user.

If you inspect your backup drive, you will notice that it is populated with several layers of folders containing your backups. On its initial backup, Time Machine does a complete backup of your machine. Then, as you work with your Mac, it makes a note of what files have been modified and creates a partial backup with only those modified files.

Time Machine automatically names the folders for each manual backup using a *year-month-date-hour:minute:seconds* scheme. Each of these backup folders contains a full version of your system so that you can easily find changes between each version when in restore mode.

Besides the manual backups, it will also create a folder called Hourly that will hold the backups that are created each hour assuming you are using the automatic backup interval.

Setting up Time Machine

Apple prides itself in Time Machine's two-step setup. The first step is to get a secondary drive. The easiest solution is to get a FireWire or USB2-powered external hard drive. It doesn't really matter what brand you use. Just ensure that it is compatible with Mac OS X (most are). If you have a tower like a Power Mac G4, Power Mac G5, or Mac Pro, you can also install a second internal hard drive to serve as your Time Machine drive. If you aren't comfortable installing hardware inside your machine, you can use an external drive as well.

Once you successfully connect the drive to your machine, Mac OS X will ask if you would like to use that drive as a backup drive (see Figure 8-1).

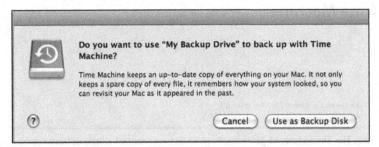

Figure 8-1. When you first connect your new drive, Mac OS X will ask whether you want to enable it as a Time Machine backup.

After selecting Enable Time Machine, the Time Machine preferences pane will load; here is where you set the other options for Time Machine. As I mentioned, Apple's focus with Time Machine is making the setup as seamless as possible. The only two options you have to set are which disk to back up time machine to and what directories or other drives on your Mac to not back up as part of Time Machine (see Figure 8-2).

Time Machine automatically runs hourly, daily, and weekly backups in the background without any user intervention. Each time Time Machine backs up your system, it is making a copy of any changed files it finds on your system disk. Having a massive copy operation running in the background can be a bit of a performance hindrance if you are running a lower-end Mac, especially if you are working on a file that is several hundred megabytes in size, such as a video file.

By default, Time Machine backs up your entire system. If you would rather not back up certain directories, you can specify that in the Options section of the Time Machine preferences pane. Here you can specify either secondary hard drives (if you have them) or folders on your main drive that you would not like included in your backups. For example, you could tell Time Machine to not back up anything in your Applications directory if you would like to save space on your drive.

8

Time Machine makes the process of managing your backup drive completely hands off if you'd like. When you are running out of disk space on the drive, it will begin deleting your oldest backups. If you want to be warned before a deletion is done, check the Warn when old backups are deleted check box under Time Machines options sheet.

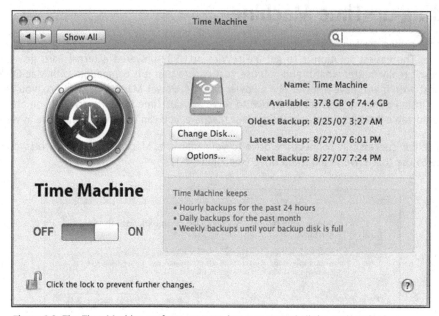

Figure 8-2. The Time Machine preferences pane lets you control all the options for how your Mac is backed up.

Going back in time

In the event that you find you need to restore your files, the process is a button click away. Navigate to your Applications folder and look for the Time Machine application. When you double-click it, your screen will be morphed into a unique view built around a cosmic background (see Figure 8-3).

The restore view shows a series of window snapshots in the middle of the window. To the right of the snapshot windows are two arrows that let you navigate between snapshots. At the bottom of the window is an action bar that has a Cancel button, an Only Show Changes button, the date and time of the currently selected snapshot, and a Restore button. The Cancel button allows you to exit Time Machine's restore view. The Only Show Changes button hides any files that haven't changed between different versions of your Time Machine backup.

The Restore button will restore the selected files or entire view to your live system. In the bottom-right corner is a vertical timeline. If you hover over one of the ticks, you will see the date and time of that snapshot so you can switch between snapshots.

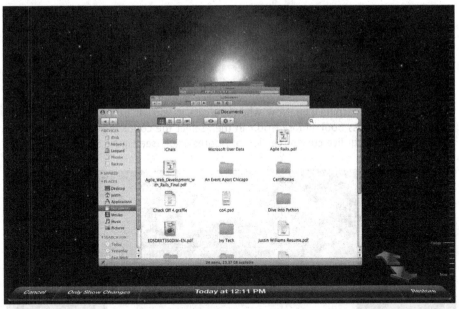

Figure 8-3. When you go to restore a file using Time Machine, your screen is morphed into a system snapshot browser built around a cosmic background.

Let's assume you want to restore a previous version of a text file. You can double-click the version of the file you think you want to restore, and a preview window will appear with the contents of the file. This works with any text document, PDF, image, or QuickTime file. If you try to preview a file in a format that isn't supported by Time Machine's restore view, it will show you an enlarged copy of the icon (see Figure 8-4).

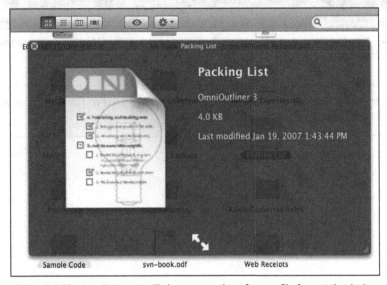

Figure 8-4. The preview pane will show you an icon for any file format that isn't supported for preview by the Time Machine restore view.

The preview window also includes two buttons at the bottom. The left button allows you to view a preview at full screen. The right button allows you to add the preview image to your iPhoto library.

You can work with Time Machine in other applications besides just the Finder. If you remove contacts from your address book and then decide you want to restore them, all you have to do is open up AddressBook and make it your frontmost application before you click the Time Machine icon. Now, when you click it, you will be shown different snapshots of your address book library. You can then select the contacts you want to restore and add them to your live current version of AddressBook (see Figure 8-5).

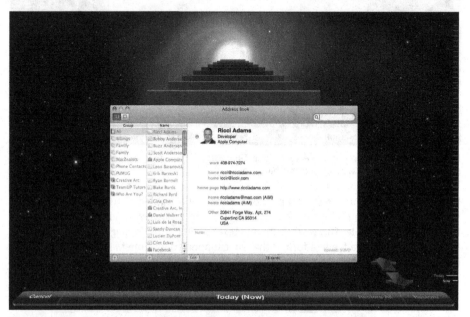

Figure 8-5. Time Machine works with any application that has had Time Machine support added into it by the developer.

> If you try to open an unsupported application like DVD Player in Time Machine, it will default to showing you snapshots of the Finder.

Summary

In this chapter, you were introduced to Apple's new backup functionality, Time Machine. I showed you how to set it up to work with your Mac and walked you through restoring files from supported applications. Time Machine is a bare-bones solution for backup, so if you are a power user, you may be longing for more. In that case, there are several great third-party backup solutions available that you may want to investigate.

In the next chapter, you'll learn more about Apple's calendaring application, iCal.

8

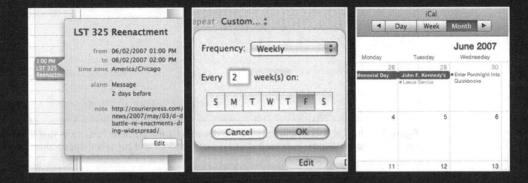

In this chapter, I will cover the following topics:

- What is iCal
- The iCalendar format
- The iCal interface
- Working with your calendars
- To do's
- Syncing your data

What is iCal

iCal, Apple's integrated calendaring solution for Mac OS X, makes it easy for you to keep track of where you need to be as well as the tasks you need to complete. Introduced back in the Mac OS X 10.2 days, Apple has left iCal rather dormant since then. With Leopard, iCal sees its most significant changes since that initial release (see Figure 9-1).

Figure 9-1. The iCal interface in Leopard is a departure from previous versions in that it no longer has a brushed metal look; instead, it sports a more modern and consistent appearance.

The iCalendar format

iCal stores its calendar data using the standard iCalendar format. By using iCalendar, iCal is able to export your calendar data out of the application as an ICS file, which can then be imported into another iCal installation or another calendaring solution like Mozilla Calendar or Google Calendar.

Each event stored in an iCalendar file is a VEVENT. A **VEVENT** defines a summary of the event, a start time, and an end time, and can also include an alarm (a **VALARM**).

Besides just support for iCal's calendar data, it also includes support for to do's, which are exported along with the calendar data. A to-do item is stored as a VTODO. A **VTODO** defines a summary and due date, and can also include a VALARM.

The iCal interface

The iCal interface, shown in Figure 9-2, is designed to be easy and accessible to a new Mac user by default. Apple has the interface split into three different columns. On the left side is your listing of calendars and a date browser. The center column holds your appointment information. The far-right column has information about the to do's you need to complete.

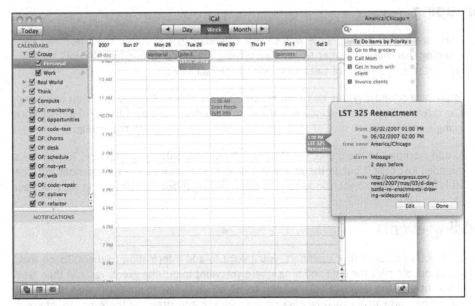

Figure 9-2. The iCal week view lets you see what is on your schedule for a week at a time.

9

iCal lets you create different calendars for each different aspect of your life. For example, you can create a calendar for your personal items and another for work items. To create a new calendar, go to the File menu and select New Calendar.

If you want to change the color or rename a calendar, choose the calendar in the listings and select Get Info from iCal's File menu. A pane will pop down that lets you adjust these values (see Figure 9-3).

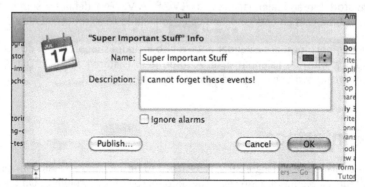

Figure 9-3. Editing calendar information is done through the Get Info pane.

Grouping

If you are one of those people with several calendars in iCal, Apple has a feature called **grouping** that makes it easier to keep everything organized. Grouping calendars basically involves storing a group of calendars under a catchall name.

To create a calendar group, go to File ➤ New Calendar Group. A group looks just like a regular calendar but has a disclosure triangle to the left of the title. Clicking the disclosure triangle enables you to hide or show the calendars associated with that group.

To add calendars to the group, just drag and drop them onto the group title. To remove a calendar, just drag it out of the group and drop it anywhere else in the calendar list. The list is fully sortable, so you can keep your calendars organized however works best for you.

Adding events

Once you've created your calendars, you'll want to add information to them. To do that, simply double-click the date and time where you want to put the event. You can then type in the title of the event. If you happen to be off by a few minutes of when the event should be, you can adjust it by clicking your mouse and dragging the event to where it belongs.

For example, if you wanted to schedule a lunch for Thursday, January 11, at noon, just double-click that date and time in your calendar. You can then rename the item from New Event, as shown in Figure 9-4, to whatever you would like to call it—Lunch, for example.

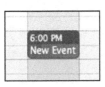

Figure 9-4.
Adding items to a calendar is as easy as double-clicking where you want to create it.

By default, scheduled items are set as one hour in length. You can adjust that size by clicking the bottom of the event and holding the mouse button down as you resize it. This will adjust the end time of the event. To adjust the start time of your event, click and drag the entire event. Time adjustments are in 15-minute increments.

If you want to add an alarm or set an event to be repeatable, you can do that by selecting an event and selecting Get Info. An event editor will appear (see Figure 9-5) that lets you adjust these values as necessary.

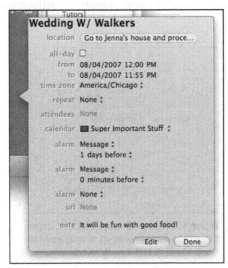

Figure 9-5. The iCal event editor lets you set additional values on your events such as alarms and attendees.

Repeatable items

If you know that every week you have a lunch date with your friend at the same time and location, you can set the item to be repeatable. By setting an item as repeatable, subsequent items will be automatically added to your calendar. To make an item repeatable, click the None text by the repeat option in your iCal drawer and select how you want to repeat the item (see Figure 9-6). Once you select your option, it will repeat that interval forever. If you know that this event should happen for only a set period of time (if you are a college student putting your semester schedule into iCal, for example), you can set the end of the period. Click the Never text and set your end date. You can either end it after so many occurrences or by a specific date.

Figure 9-6.
Events can be set as repeatable by day, week, month, or year. You can also customize the repeatability in even more fine-grained ways.

If your repeating schedule doesn't fit on the exact day every time or occurs more than once a week, you can set your repeatability to be Custom. Doing so will pop up a new view that lets you set the days you want the event to occur on and the interval to set that repeatability (see Figure 9-7). You can adjust the frequency just like before but also set the days of the week an event occurs and how often the repetition occurs (every week, two weeks, etc.).

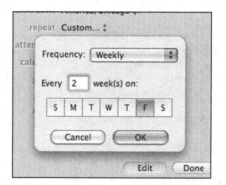

Figure 9-7. If you have an event that occurs more than once a week or month, you can easily adjust it in the Custom repeating panel.

Inviting others

iCal allows you to invite others to your event. By inviting users to your event, they will receive an e-mail with the information. To invite an attendee, click None next to the attendees label and start typing his name or e-mail address (see Figure 9-8). If the user is in your Mac OS X address book, it will give you a drop-down list of that user's associated e-mail addresses. If that user isn't in your address book, just type in his e-mail address.

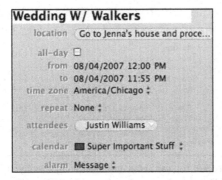

Figure 9-8. Inviting others lets you keep track of who's attending your events and who's too busy.

Once you have set all the parameters, click the Send button at the bottom of the drawer. Each invited attendee will get an e-mail with the invitation. Those who are iCal users can either accept or deny the invitation. Their response will be sent to you whether they accept or not.

Even if your attendees aren't Mac users, if they are using Google Calendar or any other iCalendar-compliant application, they can work with your iCal addresses in the same way as Mac users. Unfortunately, Microsoft Outlook and Entourage aren't compatible with the iCalendar format.

Setting alarms

If you want to be reminded before an event is scheduled to occur, you can set an alarm against it. I tend to use alarms mostly to remember appointments that I schedule far in advance, like my next dentist appointment. There are several types of alarms you can choose from. You can have an onscreen message letting you know an event is about to occur. If you have this type of alarm set, it can be synced to your iPod so you can see your message wherever you are (more on this in the section "iPod sync" later in this chapter).

You can also have an e-mail sent to you when an alarm triggers letting you know an event is to occur. You can have it sent to any of your own e-mail addresses in the Mac OS X address book.

Finally, if you are a bit more advanced, you can have a file open or run an AppleScript on an alarm triggering.

To set up an alarm, click None next to the alarm label in your iCal drawer and choose your alarm type (see Figure 9-9). Once you select the interval, you can adjust when the alarm should occur. By default, it is set to occur 15 minutes before an event is to begin.

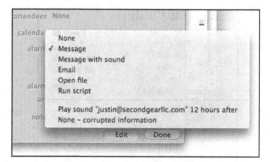

Figure 9-9. You can set alarms against any event you have in iCal.

Switching views

By default, iCal opens in the week view, but it also has support for two other views: day and month. The week view gives you an overview of everything that happens over the course of the current week. You can switch between weeks by using the arrow buttons on the endcaps of the view selector (see Figure 9-10) or by selecting a specific date in the small monthly calendar in the lower-left corner.

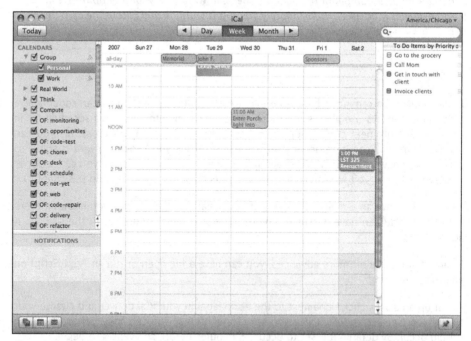

Figure 9-10. Week view lets you browse your calendar week by week to see what you have coming up in the next seven days.

The final view is the month view, which gives a monthly overview of all events happening in the current month (see Figure 9-11). Unlike the day and week views, however, it only shows the title of the event and doesn't show any time information unless you explicitly click an item and view its information in the drawer.

Figure 9-11. Month view gives you a broader overview than the other two iCal views.

Removing calendars

To remove a calendar from iCal, select the calendar from the calendar list and then select Delete from the Edit menu. If there are items associated with the calendar, a warning dialog will appear letting you know of the situation (see Figure 9-12). If you choose to delete the calendar, all calendar items and to do's associated with that calendar will be removed as well.

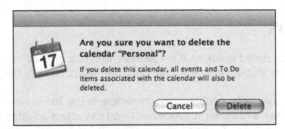

Figure 9-12. If you have any calendar events or to do's associated with a calendar, they will be deleted when you remove the calendar from iCal.

Subscribing to calendars

Besides your own calendar data, you can also subscribe to the calendar of another user, or a shared calendar. To subscribe to a calendar, you need the webcal:// address of the calendar. webcal://, the protocol associated with subscribing to iCalendar files, makes it easy to either manually subscribe inside iCal or click a link on the Web to subscribe.

Once you have the URL for your calendar, go to Calendar ➤ Subscribe. A pane will pop up allowing you to enter the address of your calendar. Once iCal finds the calendar, you can then adjust how often to update it—hourly, daily, or weekly—and whether or not you want to include the alarms and to do's that may be associated with that calendar (see Figure 9-13).

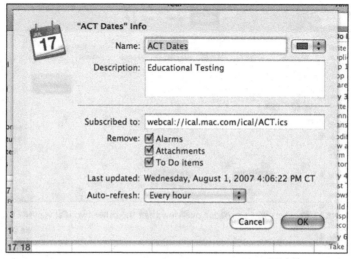

Figure 9-13. Not only can you keep your personal calendar data in iCal, but you can also subscribe to remote calendars.

If you want to find third-party calendars created by others, you can visit iCalShare at www.icalshare.com/. iCalShare has calendars for your favorite sports teams, local user group meetings, or holidays. Subscribing to a calendar is as simple as clicking the Subscribe button associated with each calendar.

Creating to do's

To do's can also be stored inside an iCal calendar. To create an iCal, make sure you have the iCal To Dos pane visible. Go to the View menu and select Show To Dos.

To create a new to-do item, double-click somewhere in the To Do view (or select File ➤ New To Do) and enter a name for it. Like events, you can access adjustable parameters by selecting File ➤ Get Info for a specific task (see Figure 9-14). You can mark an item as completed, set its priority, or specify a due date.

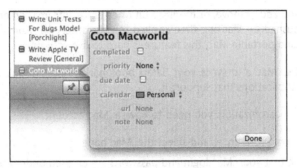

Figure 9-14. To do's have fewer customization options than iCal events, but they are useful in their own right.

By setting a priority, you can then sort your to do's list by that priority from low to high, or by title or due date, or manually. You can adjust how the items are sorted by clicking the To Do Items column header and selecting your option (see Figure 9-15).

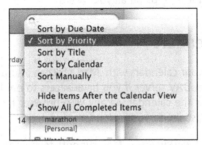

Figure 9-15. You can sort your priorities in a way that works best for you.

With Leopard, one of the best new features of iCal to do's is that they are synchronized with Mail's to do's as well. Any items you add, remove, or modify in iCal will automatically be synced with Mail (and vice versa). It will also interface with any future applications developed by Apple or third parties that interface with the calendar-related programming hooks provided by Apple.

Syncing your data

Syncing data is obviously an important feature for Mac-to-Mac calendar use or iPod-to-Mac syncing. This section will show you how to sync Mac to Mac using .Mac, how to publish your calendar, and how to sync your calendar with your iPod so you have it with you at all times.

.Mac

Besides having your iCal to do's synchronized with Apple Mail, iCal is also integrated with Apple's .Mac service so that you can synchronize your calendar data between multiple

Macs. Anytime you add, remove, or modify a bit of calendar information on one Mac, that change will be pushed to .Mac and then applied to your other Mac. For people who have both a desktop and portable Mac, this feature is hard to live without.

Besides calendars, .Mac also syncs your Safari bookmarks, AddressBook data, Keychain, and third-party applications that support it.

To enable .Mac synchronization, you need to have a .Mac account.

1. Open System Preferences and select the .Mac pane.

2. Make sure that your .Mac login and password are entered under the Account tab.

3. Go to the Sync tab and check Synchronize with .Mac. You have four options for syncing: manually, hourly, daily, and automatically.

4. Check each item that you would like to be synchronized between your Macs.

5. Click Sync Now.

You will want to perform these steps on all your Macs.

Publishing your calendars

Along with synchronizing your calendars with .Mac, you can also publish your calendars on the Web via .Mac (or a WebDAV server if you have access to one). By publishing your calendar online, you can view the calendar via any web browser through the .Mac interface or allow other users to subscribe to your calendar.

When I was in college and working as a Mac support technician for Purdue University, I kept my work schedule online and had each of my users subscribe to it via iCal, so they could see when I was in the office and when I was in class.

To publish your calendar, follow these steps:

1. Select the calendar you want to publish and then go to the Calendar menu and select Publish.

2. A pane will drop down with options for your published calendar (see Figure 9-16).

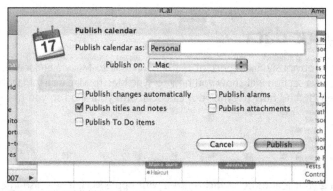

Figure 9-16. Publishing your calendar online lets you view it from any web browser, even on Windows.

3. Select Publish on: .Mac and put a check by any other option for items you want to be stored online.

4. Click Publish.

5. When your calendar is published, you have the option to visit it online and send an e-mail to users whom you want to notify of it.

iPod sync

Not only can you store your music and videos on your iPod, but you can also put your iCal and AddressBook data on there as well. By allowing iCal and AddressBook data on the iPod, Apple makes it easy to keep most of your important information with you wherever you go.

To enable syncing of your calendar and contact data, follow these steps:

1. Open iTunes and select your iPod.

2. Select the Contacts tab and check Sync iCal Calendars (see Figure 9-17) and/or Sync Address Book Contacts.

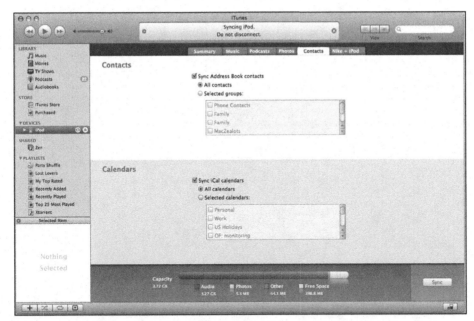

Figure 9-17. The Contacts tab is where you are able to sync your calendars and contacts with your iPod.

You can choose to sync all your contacts and calendars or only a few select ones that you want to keep with you at all times. Each time you sync your iPod, the calendar data will be updated with your iPod. Even better, if you have alarms set for events in your calendar, the alarms will trigger on your iPod.

Summary

In this chapter, I covered iCal, Apple's calendaring application. You learned how to create new calendars and associate events with them. You also saw how to customize your events to be repeatable and have alarms set against them.

You explored how to create and work with to do's in iCal and how they integrate into Apple Mail as well. You also learned how to synchronize your calendars with your iPods and .Mac.

In the next chapter, I will cover iTunes, Apple's music management application.

This chapter covers the following topics:

- Importing your music
- Editing ID3 tags and artwork
- Playlists
- Podcasts
- Burning CDs

Whenever someone mentions Apple, one of the first things that comes to mind is the success of the iPod and iTunes. iTunes is Apple's digital jukebox software for both the Mac and PC. Since its early inception back in 2001, iTunes has grown from a mere MP3 playing solution for the Mac to a full-blown media platform. Using iTunes 7, not only can you listen to music, but you can also watch videos; buy music, movies, audio books, games, and television shows; and much more. You simply go to the iTunes Store at www.apple.com/itunes/store/ to purchase them (see Figure 10-1).

Figure 10-1. iTunes 7 is Apple's media jukebox. It lets you listen to audio and view video from a single application.

Importing your music

iTunes is able to play a variety of audio files including MP3, AAC, protected AAC (purchased from the iTunes Store), and WAV files. Before you try to import these files, there are importing preferences that you may want to set. To access these settings, go to the iTunes menu and select Preferences.

In the preferences window, select Advanced. The window you see (shown in Figure 10-2) will have three tabs on it: General, Importing, and Burning.

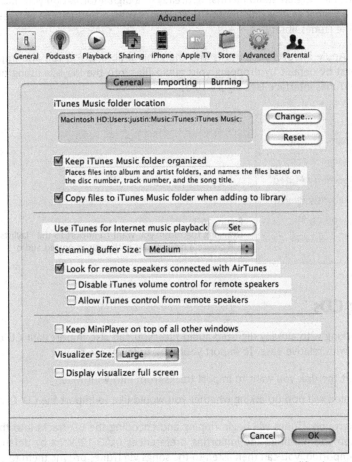

Figure 10-2. The iTunes Advanced preferences pane lets you modify where your iTunes library is stored and how to import your CDs.

The General tab lets you dictate where your iTunes library is stored and how you would like iTunes to handle your music organization. By default, Apple stores all your music inside /Users/*yourname*/Music/iTunes/iTunes Music/. I am not a fan of this layout and prefer to have the folders for each artist directly accessible from the root Music folder. To modify this, click the Change button, navigate to the Music folder, and click Choose.

You will also want to keep the options Keep iTunes Music folder organized and Copy files to iTunes Music folder when adding to library checked.

After tweaking the general preferences settings, click the Importing tab. Here you can modify how your music is encoded when you import a CD. The default values give you a balance between good audio quality and a small file size. If you are an audiophile, you can adjust the settings to be something more tuned to your ear.

Importing digital files

If you want to import an audio file that is already in a digital format on your machine, the process is as simple as dragging it into iTunes. iTunes will go through the process of copying it into the iTunes library.

By default, Apple imports your tracks into the general library. You can also import them into a playlist by default by dropping your audio files into the Playlists listing on the left side of the iTunes interface (see Figure 10-3).

Figure 10-3.
Dragging the music you want to import to the Playlists area will create a new playlist with your imported audio.

Importing CDs

Besides working with already digitized audio files, you can also import your CD collection into iTunes with relative ease. To import your CDs, follow these steps:

1. Insert the disk you want to import tracks from into your Mac.

2. A dialog will pop up asking whether you would like to import the CD. Click Yes.

In the background, iTunes will begin ripping and encoding the CD tracks into the format you set when you modified the importing preferences (AAC 128kbps by default). When your CD is imported, you can then listen to the songs via iTunes or sync them to your iPod.

Listening to your music

With all of your music imported into iTunes, you have a massive library of songs to listen to. Apple provides three ways to browse through your library and listen to those songs.

List view

List view, or classic view as I like to call it, is the default way to listen to music while working in iTunes. Each song is displayed on its own row with the artist, album, and several other pieces of metadata inline (see Figure 10-4). You can customize what fields are shown in the list by right-clicking a column header and checking what fields you would like to be visible.

Figure 10-4. iTunes' list view is chock full of data about your music, including playcounts, ratings, and more.

10

> To show or hide the Genre, Artist, Album Browser, click the eye icon at the bottom of the iTunes window.

Album view

Album view, a new view in iTunes 7, puts the album art for the song or album to the left of the information that is visible in the standard list view (see Figure 10-5). To switch into album view, go to View ➤ Album View.

Figure 10-5. Album view puts the album art for a song to the left of the album listing.

Cover Flow

Cover Flow is a unique way to view your album by its artwork (see Figure 10-6). Cover Flow view adds a black pane to the top of the list view that displays an enlarged version of the album art for each piece of music that is in your iTunes library. When you switch between songs, Cover Flow view will rotate forward or backward in a movement that is similar to changing the pages in a CD jukebox.

Besides showing your currently selected song, you can also navigate between albums by using the horizontal slider along the bottom of the Cover Flow view.

> *You can view Cover Flow in full-screen mode by clicking the button in the bottom-right corner of the Cover Flow view.*

Figure 10-6. Cover Flow view lets you navigate your music library by album art.

Editing your ID3 tags and artwork

When you see the title, artist, and album name of a track in your iTunes library, that data is pulled from the MP3's ID3 tag. **ID3** is a data container inside an MP3 or AAC file that describes the contents of the audio. By embedding this information inside the MP3 file, if you share a song with a friend, when she imports it into her iTunes library, the ID3 data would be read and displayed rather than your friend having several undescribed audio files.

Editing ID3 data

In iTunes, it's simple to edit ID3 data on one or more files at a time. ID3 tags make it easy to classify and organize your music by genre, artist, and many other different attributes. You can then use this data to create smart playlists such as one that contains just your favorite artists.

To edit ID3 tags, select the file(s) you want to modify and go to File ➤ Get Info. A window will appear that has a listing of all of the ID3 data available (see Figure 10-7).

10

Figure 10-7. ID3 tags are displayed under the Info tab.

If you are working with multiple files at a time, any field that is not common between all of the files will appear blank. If you modify the values, those changes will be applied to all selected files.

The Summary tab gives you an overview of the ID3 data that is available on the selected file. The Info tab is where you will find the most useful information. Here you can edit the available fields that are associated with the specific audio files you want to work with.

Importing album artwork

Besides editing ID3 tags, you can also associate album artwork with each MP3 file. Album artwork is viewable via album view, Cover Flow view, or by syncing it to your iPod.

There are several different ways to acquire album art. The default method is to let iTunes try to grab artwork from the iTunes Store. If Apple can match up a CD in your iTunes library with an album that is for sale on iTunes, it will download the artwork and embed it in your local copy of the song.

Unfortunately, not all music is on iTunes, and if you are a fan of obscure tunes, you may have little luck with the iTunes-embedded method. A more thorough method you could use is to employ a third-party application like CoverScout, shown in Figure 10-8, from equinux (www.coverscout.com). CoverScout will scour the Internet to find artwork for each of your songs using Google Image Search and Amazon. If you're unsuccessful after CoverScout finishes searching its sources, you also have the option of embedding an image of the album cover that you take yourself using an iSight camera.

Figure 10-8. CoverScout lets you find album art for all of your songs that aren't found in the iTunes Store.

Any song you buy from iTunes already has artwork embedded.

Working with playlists

Before the era of the MP3, people would create mixtapes with their favorite songs and share them with their friends. In the iTunes era, we create playlists. Playlists come in two flavors: regular and smart.

Regular playlist

A **regular playlist** is manually created by dragging and dropping the songs you want into it. You are the creator and maintainer of the playlist and can add and remove songs at will. To create a playlist, go to File ➤ New Playlist, enter a description for that list, and then start dragging songs into it.

Smart playlists

Smart playlists are a bit more interesting than regular playlists. A **smart playlist**, like a smart folder in the Finder, is automatically created based on a set of rules you define. For example, if you want to have a playlist of only Oasis tunes, you could create a smart playlist to accomplish it.

1. Go to File ➤ New Smart Playlist.

2. In the window that pops up (see Figure 10-9), modify the first rule to be Artist contains Arcade Fire.

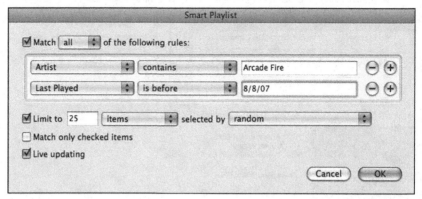

Figure 10-9. Creating a smart playlist for your favorite group will allow you to access your favorite music quickly and automatically.

3. Click OK.

You can obviously create more complex smart playlists by adding more rules to the list. For example, you could create a smart playlist that has all of your newly added music as well as tunes you haven't listened to (a playcount of 0). To do so, set up your rules so that they match Figure 10-10.

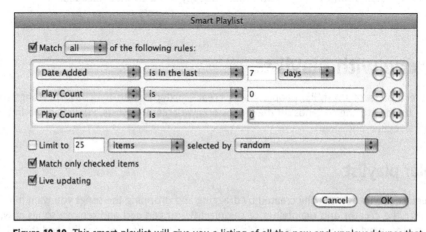

Figure 10-10. This smart playlist will give you a listing of all the new and unplayed tunes that are in your iTunes library. Never listen to the same song twice!

Podcasts

Podcasts are Internet audio shows created by people all over the world and shared via RSS. Apple added support for podcasting a few years ago when the technology was just gaining its footing. Today, podcasting has exploded, and many major organizations like ESPN and NPR have embraced it as a way to get their content out to new listeners for free.

Subscribing to podcasts

Besides selling music, movies, and television shows, Apple's iTunes Store also is the main place to find and subscribe to podcasts. To get to Apple's podcast listings, click the Podcasts item in the iTunes source list and then select Podcast directory at the bottom-right corner of the screen. This will take you to Apple's Podcast directory (see Figure 10-11).

Figure 10-11. The iTunes Podcast directory contains almost every podcast known to man. You're bound to find something you'll want to listen to in there.

Apple divides up podcasts by a variety of categories such as music, film, technology, and more. Once you find a podcast you would like to hear, click the Subscribe button to add it to your podcast listing in iTunes.

iTunes will automatically download all of the latest shows as well as give you the option to download past episodes so that you can listen to them on your Mac or sync them with your iPod.

Great Mac podcasts

If you are looking for a few podcasts to get you started, here are a few good Mac-related podcasts you can subscribe to:

- **MacBreak Weekly**: A weekly roundtable discussion about all things Mac-related with Leo Laporte, Merlin Mann, and more
- **MacCast**: A weekly news and reviews podcast by Adam Christianson
- **Cocoa Radio**: A developer interview series with some of the leading people behind the Mac software you use hosted by Blake Burris
- **Macworld**: A semiregular podcast put together by the editors of *Macworld* magazine

Burning CDs

If you don't have an iPod to sync, you can still use iTunes to burn old-fashioned audio CDs based off your playlists. iTunes, like the Finder, has built-in support for burning audio files, MP3 files, or data CDs that you can play in any disk player.

To create a CD, follow these steps:

1. Create a new playlist and add music to it.
2. If you want to burn a regular audio CD, make sure you keep the combined audio time under 80 minutes. If your CD player can support MP3 players (most modern ones can), you can throw that limit out the window.
3. Once you're happy with your playlist, click Burn Disc at the bottom of the iTunes interface.

> *If you have a CD player that supports CD text, iTunes 7 can now burn it to disk as well. You can enable it in iTunes' burning preferences.*

Backing up your iTunes

If you have a lot of music that you have either purchased or invested the time in ripping from your personal CD collection, it only makes sense that you back it up. If you are using Time Machine, your music is backed up to an external drive automatically, but it also doesn't hurt to create hard copies on DVD that you can store elsewhere such as in your office.

To create a backup of iTunes, follow these steps:

1. Go to File ➤ New Playlist.

2. A new window will pop up that gives you the option of backing up your entire library or just your iTunes purchases (see Figure 10-12). You want to make sure you at least back up your iTunes purchases since you can't redownload them from iTunes if your hard drive fails.

3. Insert a blank DVD or CD and click Back Up.

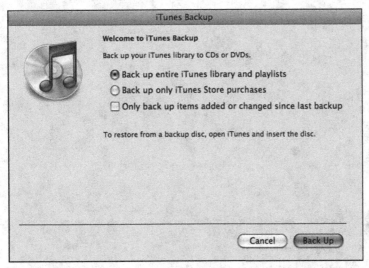

Figure 10-12. iTunes' Backup feature lets you back up your entire iTunes library or just your iTunes store purchases.

After your initial backup, you can do an incremental backup periodically that will only back up your new or changed files.

10

Summary

iTunes is a staple of the Mac platform. In this chapter, I showed you how to use it to organize and listen to your music more effectively. You learned about importing music from your CDs, browsing your library with the three different music views, and creating and managing playlists. You also learned about editing your music's ID3 tags and how to burn back up disks.

In the next chapter, I will cover the iTunes of digital photography: iPhoto.

11 iPHOTO

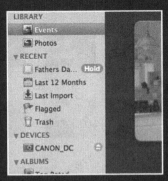  

In this chapter, I will cover the following topics:

- What is iPhoto
- Importing your photos
- Working with events
- Creating albums
- Tagging your images
- Image editing features
- Exporting your photos

iPhoto is Apple's digital photo management solution that is bundled as a part of iLife. Using iPhoto, you can import, organize, and edit your digital photographs as well as print them or publish them as part of a calendar, book, or greeting card. Behind iTunes, iPhoto is the most known and used piece of the iLife suite, as so many people these days own digital cameras.

Before iPhoto was introduced, organizing photos involved many manual processes. Users would have to import their photos via Image Capture or drag them off of a flash card to the Finder and then come up with a system for organizing the files in the Finder. After importing your photos, there wasn't much you could do with them outside of viewing them without purchasing a third-party tool like Adobe Photoshop.

With iPhoto, shown in Figure 11-1, all of that is a thing of the past.

Figure 11-1. iPhoto's all-in-one design makes it easy to work with your photos.

Importing photos

When you first launch iPhoto, you will be asked whether you want to use iPhoto as the default importer for your digital camera. Choose Yes. You can always change this setting in the future by opening the Image Capture application and modifying the default behavior in that application's preferences window (see Figure 11-2).

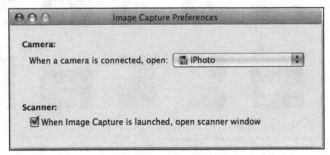

Figure 11-2. If you want to edit the default behavior when your camera is connected, you can change it in the Image Capture application's preferences.

iPhoto can import your photos either from the Finder or straight from your digital camera. Importing from the Finder is as simple as dragging photos into your iPhoto library and letting iPhoto take over from there. iPhoto will copy the images into the application's internal photo database. The iPhoto database contains all your original masters, any edited versions of your photos, and all the metadata associated with iPhoto.

> It's generally advised not to edit any of these files directly from the iPhoto library since the changes aren't synced up with the application.

If you have a digital camera, importing is even easier. The hardest step is finding your digital camera's USB cable and connecting it to your Mac. From there, iPhoto will detect your camera and add it to the Devices section of iPhoto's sidebar (see Figure 11-3). When you select your camera or card reader from the Devices section, you will see the Import panel, which is where you can define a name of the event when the photos were taken and a brief description. The event name is useful not only for metadata purposes, but also with browsing your library (more on that in the section "Browsing your library" later in this chapter). By default, iPhoto names each event with the date the photos were taken. I prefer to import my photos with the event name or subject I am shooting (Christmas, Portraits, Landscapes, etc.).

11

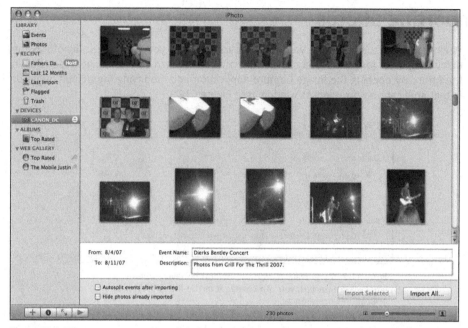

Figure 11-3. When you connect your digital camera, iPhoto will detect it automatically. No drivers to install!

Once you have defined your event name, you can also tell iPhoto to delete the images from your camera's memory card if you want to save space. With the cost of flash memory decreasing, I'd recommend keeping a copy of your photos on the flash memory card and purchasing a new card when you run out of space. If your Mac's hard drive ever fails, you will still have your photos because they were saved on those cards.

If you are going to be importing photos from multiple events at a single time, check the Autosplit events after import check box. This will check the date a photo was taken and group it by that. It may not be 100% perfect, but I'll show how you can make changes to the events iPhoto creates later in this chapter.

Browsing your library

Once you have imported your photos into iPhoto, you can browse through all of them in two different ways. At the top of the sidebar you will see two options under Library: Events and Photos. Events consolidates your photos based on when they were imported and the date they were shot (see Figure 11-4). If you double-click an event, you can view all the photos in that event.

If you just want to see all of your photos at once, you can click the Photos option under Library and see a thumbnail of each one of your photos. If you have a lot of photos in your library, iPhoto also has a way to help you quickly find what you are looking for when scrolling through your library. If you click and hold on the vertical slider to navigate through the iPhoto library, a translucent black overlay will appear with the roll name and date of import for the currently visible photos (see Figure 11-5).

Figure 11-4. The events view makes it easy to find photos for a specific time and date.

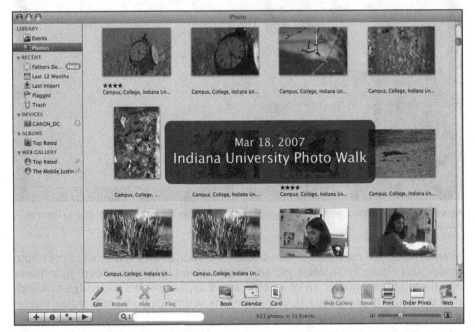

Figure 11-5. If you have a lot of images in your library, you can quickly find what you are looking for with the scrolling overlay that appears.

iPhoto lets you decide how many photos you want to see in a row by letting you dynamically resize the thumbnail using the slider in the bottom-right corner of the interface (see Figure 11-6). The farther you move the slider to the right, the larger the thumbnail will be.

Figure 11-6. The slider at the bottom of iPhoto's window lets you resize your thumbnails to a size that works best for you.

Another way to browse through your photos is iPhoto's full-screen view. Adapted from its big brother, Aperture (www.apple.com/aperture/), full-screen view takes over your entire Mac desktop with a black overlay and then puts your photos front and center (see Figure 11-7). From full-screen view, you can view your photos one by one and apply any editing techniques you see fit to the photos.

Figure 11-7. iPhoto's full-screen view lets you focus solely on your photos and manipulate them as you see fit.

To enter full-screen mode, click the Full-Screen View button on the bottom of the iPhoto window (see Figure 11-8). When you are in full-screen mode, if you hover your mouse over the top of the window, an image browser will appear that lets you navigate through all of the images in your library. Hovering along the bottom gives you edit controls that let you manipulate the currently selected image.

 Figure 11-8. iPhoto's Full-Screen View button

If you want to view images side by side, you can select multiple images by holding down the Control or Shift keys as you click them. This will line up each photo in a grid so you can view the subtle differences between multiple versions of a shot.

Working with events

Ordering by events is a great way to organize photos, and I'm a fan of letting iPhoto automatically sort my photos by the event, but sometimes it's not perfect. There are also times that I take a stray photo that I don't want to have associated with an event. For example, I like to snap photos of my dogs and organize them in their own event.

Let's say you are attending a two-day conference or family reunion. iPhoto is likely to autocreate multiple events for that single event. If you're an obsessive organizer like me, this is completely unacceptable. Luckily, it's easy to merge to events. Select one of the events and drag it on top of another. A dialog box will pop up, as shown in Figure 11-9, asking if you are sure you want to merge the two sets. Once you confirm it, the two events will be consolidated.

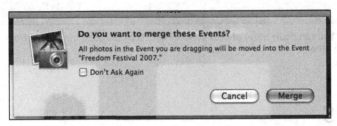

Figure 11-9. Merging events lets you keep your photos organized and easy to work with.

There are also times that iPhoto doesn't split your events exactly how you want them and instead consolidates two sets' worth of photos into a single event. If you double-click an event, you can see all of the photos associated with that event. If you see photos in that event that shouldn't be there, and instead should be in their own separate event, highlight them and click the Split button. The selected photos will be separated into their own event, and you can adjust the name and date as necessary.

If you want to move a single photo from one event to another, the best place to do that is in the photos view. Select the photo you want to move and drag it up or down until you find the event you want the photo associated with and drop it there (see Figure 11-10). The photo will be permanently moved into that event.

11

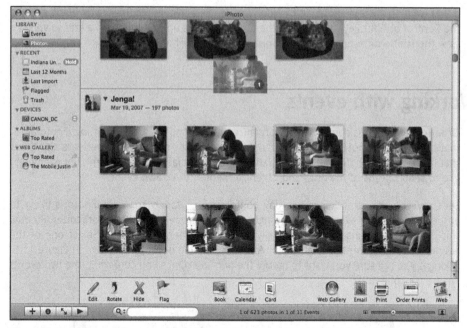

Figure 11-10. You can easily move photos between events by dragging the photos from one event section to the other.

Skimming

My favorite feature in iPhoto is **skimming**, which lets you easily scroll through the photos inside each event by just running your mouse over that event (see Figure 11-11). As your mouse moves, you will see photos that are inside that event. The faster you move your mouse, the faster the photos will scroll.

Figure 11-11.
When you run your mouse over an event, you can see a thumbnail preview of each photo inside the event.

When you aren't skimming through a group, there is a photo that is shown as the default photo for that event. If you have a favorite photo in an event you'd like to set as that photo, you can do so easily. First, click the event you want to set the photo in so that the yellow ring surrounds the event. Next, skim through the photos until you find the photo you want. When you find the photo you are interested in using, press the spacebar. Pressing the spacebar will set the currently visible photo as the default photo.

Tagging images

If you have a large photo library, being able to find that perfect shot for the occasion quickly is essential. While you could sift through your library manually, it would help if you could whittle down the results to match certain criteria. One way you can achieve this is by **rating** and **tagging** the images.

Ratings, like in iTunes, are 1–5 stars, which let you quickly locate your best (and worst) photos. To rate a photo, go to Photos ➤ My Rating and select the star rating you want to assign a photo. Alternatively, you can use the quick Cmd+0 to Cmd+5 keyboard shortcuts.

Tagging, or keywords as iPhoto calls it, is the process of assigning word(s) that describe what is going on in a photo. For example, if you have a photo of your dog, you could tag it *Dog, Animal, Pet, Bichon*.

To tag your photos with keywords, select Window ➤ Show Keywords to bring up the Keywords panel (see Figure 11-12), which gives you a listing of all the keywords currently being used in iPhoto.

Figure 11-12. The Keywords panel lets you easily tag your photos by clicking each keyword.

Select the photos you want to have tagged and then on the keyword you want to have associated with that photo or group of photos. A selected keyword will be highlighted in blue.

If you don't see the keyword you want to add to a photo in the current listing, click Edit Keywords to bring up the window shown in Figure 11-13; here you can add, edit, and rename existing keywords.

11

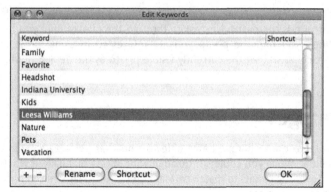

Figure 11-13. The Edit Keywords window lets you manipulate the keywords you can use in iPhoto.

If you want a quicker way to add and edit keywords, you can add them inline below the rating in a photo, as shown in Figure 11-14, by typing the keyword and then pressing the comma key (,).

Figure 11-14.
If you want to quickly add and remove keywords from a photo, you can type them out below the ratings in the photos view.

Albums

Like iTunes' playlists, iPhoto supports both regular and smart albums to organize your photos.

Regular albums

A **regular album** is manually created by dragging and dropping the photos you want included into it. You are the creator and maintainer of the playlist and can add and remove photos at will. To create an album, go to File ➤ New Album, enter a description, and then start dragging photos into your new album.

Smart albums

A **smart album** is automatically created based on a set of rules you define. For example, if you wanted to have an album of all your highest rated photos, you could create a smart album to accomplish it. To do so, follow these steps:

1. Go to File ➤ New Smart Album.

2. In the window that pops up (see Figure 11-15), modify the first rule to be My Rating is greater than 3 stars.

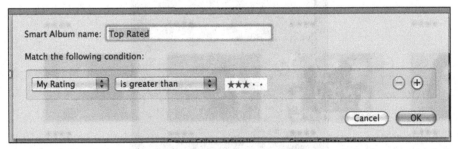

Figure 11-15. Creating smart albums lets you automatically organize your photos based on a set of defined criteria.

3. Click OK.

Besides ratings, keywords, file names, and dates, you can also create a smart album based on information such as a photo's aperture, camera model, or shutter speed by adjusting the criteria in the first pull-down menu on the smart album (see Figure 11-16).

Figure 11-16. A smart album is automatically updated as new photos meet the criteria.

Editing images

iPhoto includes basic editing tools for working with your photos. Using iPhotos tools, you can do things such as crop and rotate your photos, apply photo effects (black and white, sepia tone, etc.), or adjust the exposure and levels. You can do all of this from the Adjust panel (see Figure 11-17).

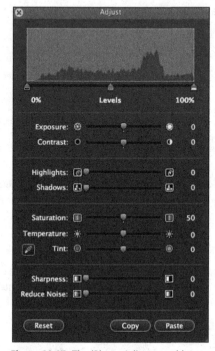

Figure 11-17. The iPhoto Adjust panel lets you modify how your photos look.

To edit a photo, select it and then click the Edit button. From there, the iPhoto toolbar will show a listing of the tools available to you. If you want more fine-grained image editing support, you can use a third-party editor such as Adobe Photoshop to edit your photos. When using an external editor, you are in essence just using iPhoto as a photo organization tool.

Double-clicking a photo will launch it in Photoshop. When you are finished editing the photo and save your changes, they will be applied back to the iPhoto library.

To enable external editor support, follow these steps:

1. Open iPhoto's preferences.

2. In the Main tab, change the Edit Photo pull-down menu setting to In Application.

3. In the window that pops up, select your external editor.

Exporting to Flickr

iPhoto supports a variety of ways to share and export your photos. You can create a calendar with your 12 favorite photos or a book that you can share with friends and family, or export your photos to your .Mac account. The process for each of these is intuitive and easy to do, so I won't bother covering it in this book.

What isn't built into iPhoto is the ability to export photos to Flickr in an easy and intuitive way. Luckily, Connected Flow has created the FlickrExport plug-in for iPhoto (www.connectedflow.com/flickrexport/). You can purchase a license for this plug-in from the Connected Flow site.

In case you don't know, Flickr is the social photo-sharing site owned by Yahoo that lets you upload your photos as well as leave comments on your friends' photos. Once installed, FlickrExport resides in the Export Photos panel of iPhoto (which you can access by selecting File ➤ Export).

As you can see in Figure 11-18, the FlickrExport interface supports uploading multiple photos as well as adding metadata such as a title, a description, and tags. If you have your photos tagged or titled in iPhoto, FlickrExport is smart enough to read that data in by default for your photos that will be uploaded.

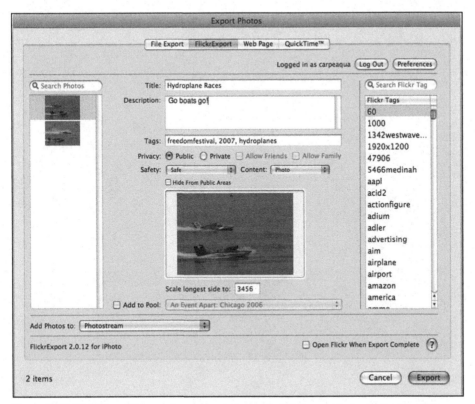

Figure 11-18. FlickrExport lets you share your photos on the Flickr.com photo-sharing site easily from within iPhoto.

To upload a photo to Flickr using FlickrExport, follow these steps:

1. Select one or more photos.
2. Go to File ➤ Export.
3. Select the FlickrExport tab.
4. Modify the tags, title, and description for each photo to fit your needs.
5. Click Export.

Summary

In this chapter, you learned how to work with digital photos using iPhoto. I showed you how to import photos from your digital camera into iPhoto. You learned how to work with and manipulate events in iPhoto. You also saw how to organize photos using ratings and keywords so you could create things like smart albums to easily find your photos. Finally, I covered adjusting your photos and exporting them to Flickr.

In the next chapter, I will cover iMovie and iDVD, Apple's two iLife applications that work with digital video.

12 iMOVIE AND iDVD

If you have a video camcorder, you probably have a lot of family videos or other types of footage that you have shot. While it's OK to just watch the tape straight through, it's nothing compared to the power of taking that footage, adding some music and transitions to it, and watching a completed piece of work that you put together. iMovie makes that happen.

The earliest of the iLife apps, iMovie made its introduction in 1998 with the original iMac. At the time, home digital video editing wasn't really popular, but with the low-priced iMac and iMovie, Apple aimed to change that, and they did. Using iMovie in line with a digital video camcorder gives you the perfect balance between an easy-to-use consumer editing application and a professional tool. In fact, at a previous job, many of our video editors used iMovie for producing videos when they felt Final Cut was too powerful.

Importing your footage

Obviously, the first step to working with iMovie is shooting some video. Go out and do that first. Once you have your footage, grab your FireWire cable, connect your camera to your Mac, and open the iMovie application. You'll see the iMovie interface take up your entire screen, as shown in Figure 12-1.

Figure 12-1. iMovie uses an all-in-one interface to store your video clip, edit your movie, and export it to various formats.

Like the other iApps, the iMovie interface is all-inclusive. In other words, everything is contained in a single window. The application is segregated into two major sections. The bottom of the application is focused on your video library, which archives all the footage you pull from your camcorder and organizes it by date and event. The top of the interface focuses on the current video project you are working on. To the left is a listing of the projects you've created in iMovie, the middle focuses on the selected project's timeline, and the right focuses on a preview of the movie.

To import video from your camera, you simply click the Camera Import button (with the camcorder icon) on the left side of the iMovie screen. This brings up the Import window, as shown in Figure 12-2, which lets you begin importing the video into iMovie. If you want to import an entire tape without any intervention, move the slider on the left from Manual to Automatic. If you want to control playback of your camcorder and importing from iMovie, slide it to Manual.

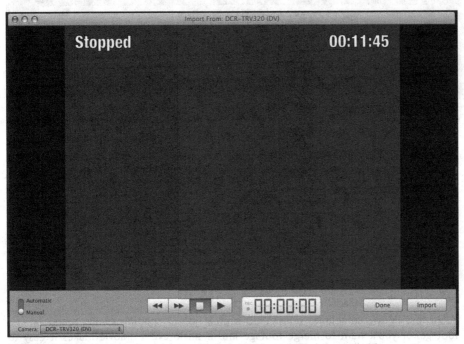

Figure 12-2. The Import window lets you see what video is currently being pulled from your camcorder.

When you click the Import button, you will be prompted to add your video to a new event or an existing one. Events are used by iMovie to organize your video into logical folders that you can browse via iMovie. You will also have the option of saving the video to your Mac's hard drive or an external FireWire drive.

As the video is importing, you will see the clips and audio through the preview window. When you are done importing your video, simply click the Import button again.

12

> *Unfortunately, iMovie only supports a single video and audio track. If you need more than one video or audio track, you will need to use Final Cut Express or Final Cut Pro.*

Browsing your video library

Once you've imported your clips into the library, you can browse them via the video library (see Figure 12-3). The left side of the video library shows you all your events sorted by dates. Clicking an event lets you see all of the video that is included as part of that event.

Figure 12-3. The video library lets you browse all your video clips and add them to your different movie projects.

You can adjust how often a preview clip is shown in the library. To do so, adjust the slider in the lower-right corner of the iMovie window (see Figure 12-4). I tend to leave mine at 5s (5 seconds).

Figure 12-4. The video library slider lets you adjust how often a preview clip is shown in the video library.

You'll find iMovie sometimes doesn't do a great job at splitting events based on the footage, or you'll want to merge footage into a single event. iMovie makes it easy to organize your events. If you want to combine the clips of two events, you can easily do so by dragging one of the events onto the other.

Skimming

When you want to find an exact clip to use in your movie project, you can quickly do so using skimming. **Skimming** is the process of moving your mouse along a clip of video and seeing a preview of what the clip contains. Skimming a clip plays it at the speed of your mouse movement, so if you want to quickly run through a set of clips, just move your mouse along it quickly.

Skimming is great if you've shot a lot of video and are quickly looking for clips. You can skim an entire library in a few minutes.

Creating a movie project

After you have imported all of your raw video footage into iMovie, you can start the process of creating a movie. The first thing you will need to do is create a project. To do so, follow these steps:

1. Select File ➤ New Project.
2. In the pane that appears, name the project and select the aspect ratio you want your video to be formatted in.
3. Select Create.

Editing your movie

Once your project is created, you'll have a blank project timeline like the one in Figure 12-5.

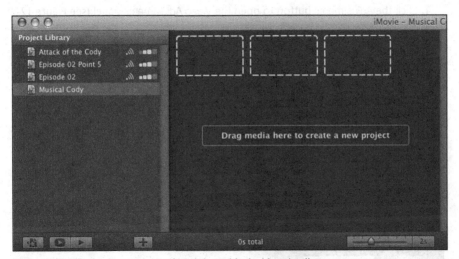

Figure 12-5. When you create a project, it has a blank video timeline.

iMovie makes it easy to create a movie with minimal effort. To start adding clips to your movie, just follow four easy steps:

1. Skim through your video library to find the clip you want to use.
2. Click the section of the video you want to be the beginning point of your clip.

3. Resize the yellow rectangle (see Figure 12-6) to highlight the entire piece of video you want to be part of your movie.

Figure 12-6. The yellow rectangle that highlights your video clip lets you dictate the length of the clip you want to add to your project.

4. Drag the clip onto the project where it says "Drag media here."

Repeat the preceding process for each piece of video you want added to your movie.

Splitting clips

If you have a large clip that is almost perfect, save for a small part in the middle, iMovie allows you to split the clip and remove a portion of it. To do this, highlight the portion of the clip you want to cut out of your project in the project view (not in the video library).

Next, go to Edit ➤ Split Clip. This will splice the clip into two separate clips. The first clip contains all content up to the point of your playhead. The second clip is everything from that point on.

Adjusting your video

Sometimes the video you shoot is great footage, but the coloring is off just a bit. Like a photograph, you can do some postprocessing on the video you output to adjust things like color, white balance, and exposure. To do this in iMovie, follow these steps:

1. Click the Adjustments button to open the Video Adjustments panel (see Figure 12-7).
2. Select the clip you want to perform your adjustments on in your timeline.
3. Make adjustments as necessary in the Video Adjustments panel.
4. Click Done to save your changes or Revert To Original to undo them.

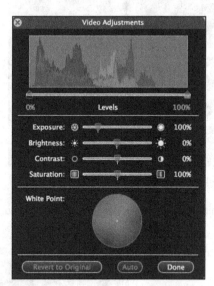

Figure 12-7.
The Video Adjustments panel lets you adjust the video's white balance, brightness, and exposure to fit your needs.

Adding audio to your movie

When you add a video clip to your timeline, it automatically imports the vocal track that is associated with that clip into your movie. If you'd like to add a music bed to your film, you can do so as well. iMovie, like the other iLife applications, is connected with your iTunes library, so you can easily embed any music that you have there inside a movie. To access your library, click the Music Tab button (with the musical note icon) on the right side of the iMovie screen.

The Music tab, along with displaying your iMovie clips, also contains sound effects and songs you may have composed in GarageBand. To add an audio clip to your movie, follow these steps:

1. Select the clip from either iTunes or the sound effects library in iMovie.

2. Drag the clip on top of the clip you want to associate it with. If you want the audio to play across the entire movie, drag it where there isn't a clip so the project timeline's background is green.

If you are in timeline view, you will see the audio clip just below your video, as shown in Figure 12-8. You can then adjust its location more granularly.

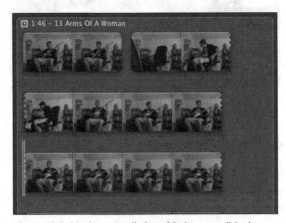

Figure 12-8. Music can easily be added to your iMovie video directly from iTunes.

Importing audio works for regular MP3s as well as songs purchased from iTunes.

Let's say you wanted to remove the audio track from some video so that only your music was playing in the background. Doing this is easy as well:

1. Open the Audio Adjustments panel (see Figure 12-9).

2. Select the clip(s) you want to have adjusted.

3. Reduce the volume to 0%.

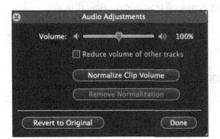

Figure 12-9.
Disabling an audio track is as easy as setting its volume to 0%.

Titles and transitions

After adding clips and music to your film, you may also want to add opening and closing credits to it just like they do in Hollywood. iMovie makes it easy to add several different types of title screens like this under the Titles Browser. The Titles Browser gives you a listing of all the available title styles that you can use in your movie (see Figure 12-10).

Figure 12-10. The Titles Browser lets you choose from several different titling styles for your movies.

To add a title to your movie, follow these steps:

1. Select a title in the list of available title styles.
2. Drag it to the place in the movie timeline where you want it to appear. If you want it to overlay a clip, drag it on top of the clip.
3. Adjust the text values to be what you want: "My Fantastic Movie," for example.
4. Adjust the color and font styles to your liking.

If you want to adjust the speed of how fast your titling appears on the screen, hover over the clip in the movie timeline and click the small clock icon in the lower-left corner. A pane will appear that lets you adjust the duration of the clip.

After you add titles to your film, one of the last things you will want to do before your film is complete is add some transitions between your clips. By default, when your movie shifts from one clip to the next, there is a quick segue between the clips. While this is fine when working with quick dialog, it's not necessarily a great way to transition between scenes.

For those times, iMovie has several different types of transitions available.

Adding a transition is similar to adding titles or effects to your film. Once inside the Transitions Browser (next to the Titles Browser), follow these steps:

1. Select a transition in the list of available transition styles.
2. Drag the transition from the transition style list to your timeline between the two clips you want transitioned.

When you add a transition or effect, you will see almost instantaneous results when you preview your movie. This is thanks to Real Time Effects & Core Video, which lets you apply effects to video by layering them on top of the base clip. While you are seeing the instantaneous results in your preview, in the background your actual video is rendering. You can't export your video until everything is finished rendering.

Exporting to the Web

The last step to creating a movie is exporting that film. iMovie supports several different formats for exporting: QuickTime, iTunes, YouTube, and .Mac. Apple and Google have developed a partnership over the previous year, and one of the fruits of this partnership is the connection between several Apple products such as the iPhone and iMovie with YouTube.

To export your finished project to YouTube, do the following (see Figure 12-11):

1. Go to the Share menu and select YouTube.
2. Next to Accounts, click the Add button to associate iMovie with your YouTube account.
3. Once connected to your account, you can title, tag, and describe your video.
4. Under Size to publish select Medium.
5. Click Next followed by Publish to send your video to YouTube.

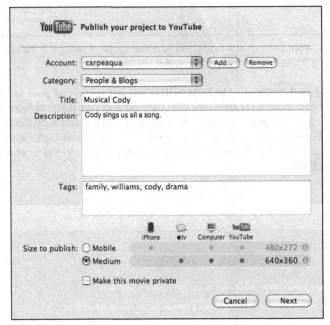

Figure 12-11. iMovie allows for direct publishing of your finished movies to YouTube.

The process of exporting to .Mac and iTunes follows a similar set of steps, so you shouldn't have any issue repeating the preceding process for those options in the Share menu.

Exporting to iDVD

If you aren't the type to share your video online, you can still use Apple's iDVD application. iDVD allows you to create and burn DVDs that you can play back on another computer or a stand-alone DVD player.

You can export to iDVD directly from iMovie by following these steps:

1. Go to the Share menu and select Export Movie.

2. In the pane that pops up, select Large as the size (see Figure 12-12). Since you are going to show this on a TV, you want the highest quality you can get.

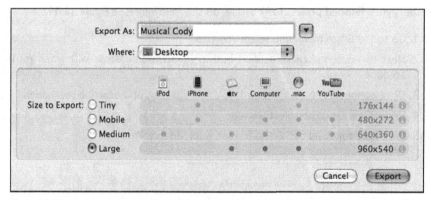

Figure 12-12. When you export a movie, you have the option of saving it in various sizes for various platforms such as the iPod, AppleTV, and YouTube.

After exporting your movie, you can open iDVD and begin creating your project. The first thing you will need to do is create a new iDVD project and save it somewhere on your hard drive. The main portion of the iDVD window will give you a preview of the theme you are using as well as the buttons that are associated with your movie (see Figure 12-13). You can modify your theme by clicking one of the available themes in the sidebar on the right side of the application.

Figure 12-13. iDVD provides an easy way to create professional-looking DVDs that you can play anywhere.

If you want to add DVD-ROM contents that can be viewed only on a computer, go to Advanced ➤ Edit DVD-ROM Contents.

Adding movie clips

Once you've selected your themes and set up your drop zones, you can go about adding your movie clips to the iDVD. To do so, follow these steps:

1. Go to the Project menu and select Add Movie.
2. A drop will appear in iMovie called Add Movie Here. Drag the file you saved from iMovie on top of this.

Adding music

Some themes come with music, while others are silent. You can change this by adding your own music to your movie. To do this, follow these steps:

1. Go to the Media tab.
2. Select the Audio tab to show your iTunes library.
3. Find the song you want in your iTunes library and click Apply.

12

Previewing your DVD

Once you have selected a theme that you like, you can get a full preview of your DVD in the DVD Player application by clicking the Play button. Your movie will open in DVD Player, and you can work with it as if it were in a regular DVD player (see Figure 12-14).

Figure 12-14. Preview mode lets you view your iDVD project as if it were being broadcast on a television or another computer.

Burning your DVD

Once you're satisfied with the look of your DVD, the last step in the process is burning it to a DVD. To do this, simply click the Burn button at the bottom of the iDVD window (see Figure 12-15). iDVD will prompt you for a blank DVD-R and will take over from there.

Figure 12-15.
When you are ready to burn your DVD, push this button.

Summary

In this chapter, I covered how to make movies on your Mac using iMovie and iDVD. You read about importing video from your digital camcorder and browsing through the video library. You learned how to create a new project and build a movie in that project by dragging clips, title, and transitions onto it.

You also saw the various ways you can export your movie from iMovie, including YouTube and iDVD.

In the next chapter, I will cover GarageBand, an iLife app that lets you create original music on your Mac.

12

13 GARAGEBAND

GarageBand is the oddball of the iLife suite. Each of the other applications seem to work with another type of data. iPhoto works with digital photos you have snapped, iMovie your movies, iTunes your music, and iWeb all of these. GarageBand is different in that it doesn't necessarily work with your other data. Instead, you create content using GarageBand.

Using GarageBand, you can create original music using **loops**, which are repeatable pieces of music. You work with loops by dragging them into the timeline and layering them on top of each other to build an **ensemble**. GarageBand includes thousands of loops, and you can purchase more from either Apple or a third party.

Additionally, Apple has built-in support for creating your own podcasts using GarageBand. You can do a one-man show or a morning zoo with your best friends, as GarageBand can record your iChat audio conversations and import them into the application. As you can see in Figure 13-1, besides vocal audio, you can also add jingles, loops, and iTunes music to your podcast.

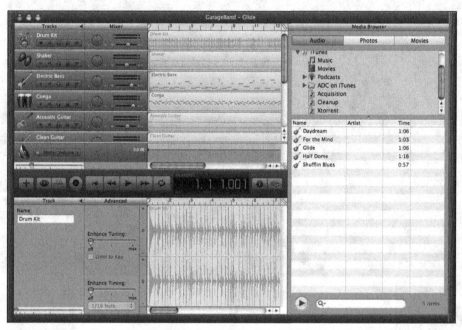

Figure 13-1. GarageBand, with its wood-grained edging, features the most unique interface of any of the iLife suite.

Figure 13-1 shows the unique GarageBand interface. On the right and left side of the application are wood grain–style edges, which aren't seen anywhere else on the Mac. The main part of the interface displays your **loop layers**. This is where you drag your loops or vocal tracks to arrange your recording. Each separate track has its own row, which can also have its own balance, volume, and more.

At the bottom of the interface is either your available loops or the chapter listing for your podcast. To the right is the Media Browser: a staple of the iLife applications. The Media Browser lets you add in photos from iPhoto or Aperture, iTunes music, or previously created GarageBand tunes.

Creating original music

If you want to use GarageBand to create an original tune, open up the GarageBand application. When launched, you will see a screen like Figure 13-2. You are given the option of creating a new music project, a podcast, or a movie score, or opening an existing file.

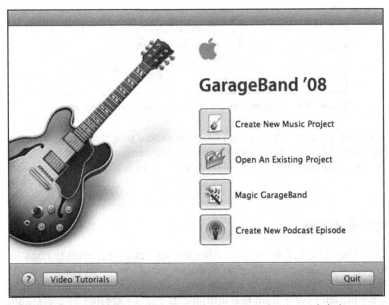

Figure 13-2. When you first launch GarageBand, you are given several choices as to what types of things you can do with the application.

Select Create New Music Project. This will open up a new window that lets you save the file to your Mac and adjust the tempo, key, and time of the song. Leave everything at the default levels unless you are sure what you are doing and then click Create (see Figure 13-3). This will open up the main GarageBand window where you will be creating your song.

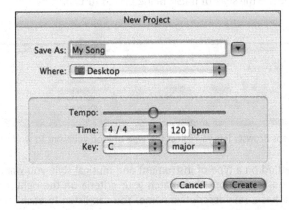

Figure 13-3. When you choose to create a new music project, you are given the option of adjusting the tempo and key of the song.

13

Tickling the ivories

When the main application window launches, you are given a single track, the Grand Piano, and are shown a piano keyboard (see Figure 13-4). If you click its keys, you can play some notes. Unfortunately, this isn't too useful on its own, as you can't easily compose something with mouse clicks.

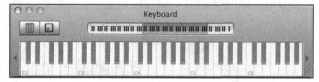

Figure 13-4. The Grand Piano lets you play tunes using your mouse.

If you had a USB keyboard (the musical type), you could plug that into your Mac, and the Grand Piano interface would be much more useful. Unfortunately, most people don't have this, so for this example just close the Grand Piano window and move on to creating your song.

The Loops Browser

If you aren't musically inclined or don't have the necessary equipment to hook up instruments to your Mac, GarageBand has an extensive set of loops that you can use to create music. Loops can be anything from a drum beat or guitar riff to a full section of horns. All loops Apple provides come from real instruments and are created by professional musicians in a studio environment, so they have nothing but the best quality sound.

To open the Loops Browser, click the eye icon in the bottom-left corner of the GarageBand window (see Figure 13-5).

As you can see in Figure 13-6, the Loops Browser divides all of GarageBand's loops into different categories based on the type of instrument and the style of music being played (urban, rock, etc.).

Figure 13-5. The Loops Browser icon is an eye.

Figure 13-6. The Loops Browser lets you select the type of loop you want to work with.

Once you have settled on a type of instrument and musical style you want to add to your track, you will see a list of loops that match your criteria on the right side of the Loops Browser. Each one has a semidescriptive name. You can listen to each loop by clicking it. The loop will play repeatedly until you click away from it or select another loop.

When you have finally settled on a loop that you are happy with, you can add it to your GarageBand track by dragging it from the Loops Browser to the desired position in your song.

The loop will only play as long as the loop is (usually 1–4 seconds). You can extend a loop by dragging either end of the loop to your desired length. It functions just like adjusting the time frame of an iCal event, only horizontally.

With a single loop added, you can preview your song by clicking the Play button in the middle of the GarageBand window. Your song probably isn't too interesting at this point, so add a few more loops by dragging different instruments onto your song's timeline and adjust them to your liking (see Figure 13-7).

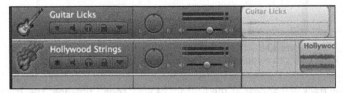

Figure 13-7. After adding a track to your song, it will appear in its own row.

Importing iTunes

Since GarageBand is part of the iLife suite, it easily interfaces with the other applications in the suite, mainly iTunes. If you wanted to use one of your favorite songs as the base for your GarageBand production, you can easily do that by dragging the song into GarageBand by following these steps:

1. Show the media manager by clicking the Media Manager icon (see Figure 13-8).

Figure 13-8. The media manager is accessible from GarageBand, so you can import other types of media into your GarageBand productions.

2. The media manager will slide open. Select the Audio tab.

3. Find the song you want to add and drag it onto your song's timeline below the other instruments.

4. Adjust its position as necessary.

13

Adding a vocal track

If you have singing skills (or if you pretend you do), you can record an audio track as part of your GarageBand track. All new Macs, save for the Mac Pro and Mac mini, come with a built-in microphone.

To add an audio track, follow these steps:

1. Select Track ➤ New Track.

2. In the pane that pops down (see Figure 13-9), select Real Instrument Track.

○ **Software Instrument Track**
For Instrument sounds created by GarageBand and playable using a USB, MIDI, or onscreen keyboard.

◉ **Real Instrument Track**
For audio recordings such as voice, guitar, bass, or any instrument that can be captured by a microphone.

Cancel   Create

Figure 13-9. After you select New Track from the Track menu, you can record either a real instrument or a MIDI keyboard.

3. A new track will appear at the bottom of your song's timeline. The Track info pane will also appear so you can add effects as necessary.

4. In the Track info pane, select Vocals, followed by male or female vocals as necessary. You can also try a different effect if you wish.

5. Click the Record button at the bottom of GarageBand's window and start wailing.

Exporting your song

Once you have a song you are proud of, you can export it in a variety of ways. You can send it to iTunes to listen to on your iPod or Mac, send it to an iWeb project, or save it to your disk. GarageBand saves tracks as AAC files.

To export your song, go to the Share menu (see Figure 13-10) and select the export option you are interested in.

ol **Share** Window Help

Send Song to iTunes
Send Podcast to iWeb
Send Movie to iDVD

Export Song to Disk...

Burn Song to CD

Figure 13-10.
GarageBand lets you export songs to iTunes, iWeb, iDVD, or your Mac's desktop as an AAC file.

Creating a podcast

If you have always aspired to have your own radio show, creating a podcast in GarageBand may just scratch that itch. To create a podcast, select Create New Podcast Episode from the GarageBand introduction window that I show again here for your convenience in Figure 13-11.

Figure 13-11. The GarageBand introduction window

Like before, you will be asked where to save your file. You won't have the option to adjust tempo or key since you aren't creating a piece of music.

The layout of the podcast creation window is altered slightly from the window for music creation (see Figure 13-12). The Loops Browser shows a column view that has sound effects and jingles rather than music loops. These are all pieces of audio that you can use to give your podcast sound some polish. Also different is the Podcast Track instrument at the top of the timeline. This is where you can add chapter art for your podcast (more on that in the section "Adding chapters" later in this chapter).

13

Figure 13-12. The Podcast creation screen

Recording your audio

The first thing you will want to do for creating your podcast is record your audio. By default, two audio tracks are created: male and female. Depending on your sex, click your appropriate track. The reason for separate tracks is that Apple has adjusted how your microphone input is filtered into the podcast based on your voice.

Once selected, click the Record button in the middle of the GarageBand interface and start talking.

When you're finished with everything you have to say, click the Record button again to stop recording your audio.

Adding background audio

You could end your podcast right now, but it wouldn't be very interesting. That's not to say that your content is boring. It's merely that most podcast listeners are used to hearing an introductory jingle and maybe a music bed just like they would on the radio. You can add these in GarageBand easily.

Let's first add a jingle from the jingles that are bundled with GarageBand (see Figure 13-13). Click the Loop Browser button (the eye icon) if you don't see the jingles.

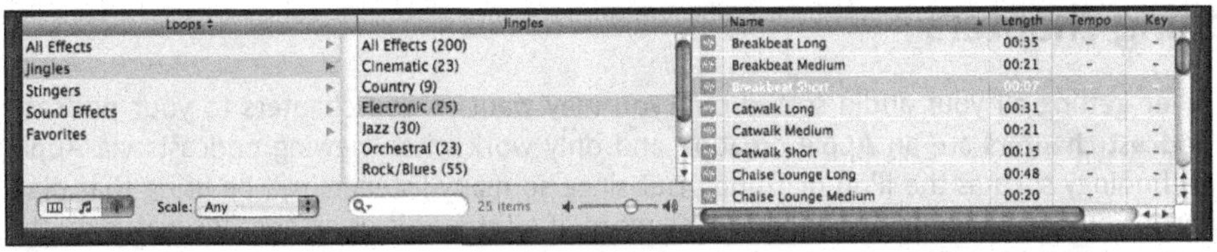

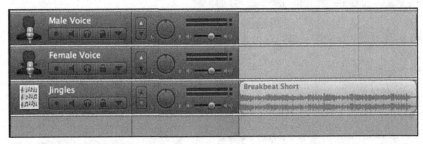

Figure 13-13. The Loops Browser for a podcast contains jingles, sound effects, and stingers.

The first thing you need to do is add an introductory jingle to your podcast. To do this, follow these steps:

1. Click Jingles from the podcast loop editor.

2. Select the music genre you want to choose from.

3. Preview clips by clicking them. When you find one you are satisfied with, drag it to the Jingles track at the beginning of your podcast's timeline (see Figure 13-14).

Figure 13-14. Once you add a jingle, you will probably want to drag your voice track to the end of that jingle.

The last piece of music you may want to add is background music. This music is played quietly in the background to bring a bit of ambience to the audio. To do this, follow these steps:

1. Click the Media Browser icon and select the Audio tab.

2. Pick a song from your iTunes library.

3. Drag it onto the timeline below the other existing tracks.

The song you choose will be imported into your project. The problem will be that your track is imported at full volume. This is a bit loud and distracting when working with the spoken word, so you need to lower the volume.

Each track has a volume slider as you can see in Figure 13-15. Drag it to the left so that your audio is just audible enough and not distracting from your voice.

Figure 13-15. Each track has a volume slider to let you adjust that specific track volume. This is called **ducking**.

13

Adding chapters

After getting all your audio sorted out, you may want to add chapters to your podcast. **Podcast chapters** are an Apple creation and only work when viewing podcasts via Apple technology such as the iPod or iTunes, but since so many listeners will be using that platform, you should be fine using it. What's more, if a listener is using another platform, the audio will play just fine: that user just won't have chapters.

To add chapter art, go to the Photos tab under the Media Browser and add the images to the podcast where you see fit. Each photo you add will create a new chapter. You can resize each photo container's length to match how long you want that chapter to last (see Figure 13-16).

Figure 13-16. Adding chapter artwork to the Podcast Track

After adding all your chapters to your podcast, you can edit the chapter titles by clicking the Track Editor button (with the scissors icon). Make sure you have Podcast Track selected, and you should see a screen like Figure 13-17.

Time	Artwork	Chapter Title	URL Title
◇ 00:00:00.000		Introduction	Second Gear
◇ 00:00:10.625		Welcome	Second Gear
◇ 00:00:18.000		Title	Second Gear

Figure 13-17. The chapter editor lets you add titles and URLs for each chapter.

The chapter editor lets you add a chapter title and a URL title and address. The URL information will appear on top of your chapter art and allow the user to click through to a web page you may have mentioned during your podcast.

The last step of your podcast creation is to add episode art. This is the album art for the specific podcast. You can do this by dragging an image to the Episode Artwork droplet in the track editor (see Figure 13-18).

Figure 13-18. Episode artwork shows up in iTunes or your iPod as the album art for your podcast.

Exporting your podcast

After your podcast is complete, you will need to export it out of GarageBand so that it can be encoded as an AAC file and distributed to your listeners. The export options for a podcast are the same as those for a regular song: iTunes, iWeb, iDVD, and your hard disk.

To export your podcast, go to the Share menu (see Figure 13-19) and select the export option you are interested in.

Figure 13-19.
Exporting a podcast is the same as with a regular song in GarageBand.

13

Summary

In this chapter, I covered GarageBand, Apple's music and podcast creation application. You saw how to create an original song with GarageBand. You also learned how to create a podcast, add chapter art, and export it so you can share it with others.

In the next chapter, I will cover iWeb, the web development application that connects all the other iLife applications together.

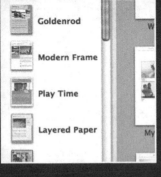

iWeb is the newest iLife application and brings the entire suite home. Using iWeb, you can publish a web site that shows off your photos, videos, and podcasts. You can also use iWeb to pen your own weblog. iWeb is based on the same technology as Apple's Safari web browser, WebCore. In Mac OS X Tiger, Apple added editing support to its browser rendering engine so that developers could create WYSIWYG (what you see is what you get) web editors similar to Adobe Dreamweaver or Microsoft Expression.

Unlike those two applications, iWeb aims to be easy to use and accessible to all users like other iLife applications.

Creating your site

When you first launch iWeb, you will see a list of all of the available templates that Apple has bundled with the application (see Figure 14-1). These templates are professionally designed and attractive. Each template also includes different page styles for static pages, an About Me page, media pages, and blog or podcast listings.

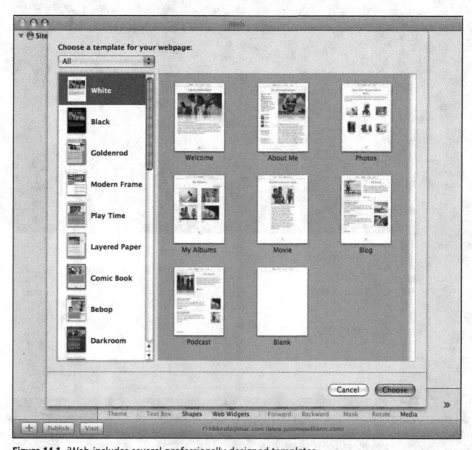

Figure 14-1. iWeb includes several professionally designed templates.

Once you find a template you are happy with, select the Welcome page and click Choose. The template will be imported into your iWeb project. On the left will be a listing of all the pages that are a part of your project. The page you selected will be shown on the right in the main content area.

Working with iWeb is incredibly easy. Just double-click a piece of text, and you can edit it to your liking. If you want to move a piece of the design around, you can click it and drag it to your desired position. As you can see in Figure 14-2, the default page has some dummy text and placeholder images. Now you'll see how to replace that with your own data.

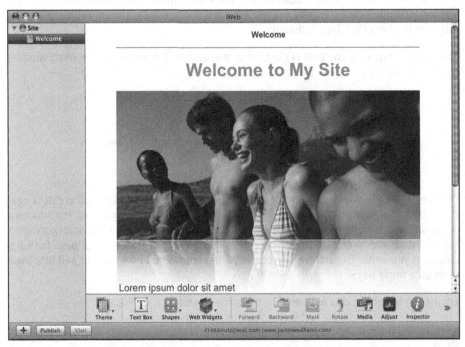

Figure 14-2. The default Welcome page template in iWeb has placeholder text and images. You can change that to display your own data easily.

Editing most of the text is intuitive, as already mentioned. The one bit of text that may give you trouble is the headline at the top of the page ("Welcome"). To modify that, you need to rename the page in the Site Organizer on the left. Just double-click the name and modify it as you like.

To tweak the image, you can use the Media Browser to select a photo from iPhoto or Aperture.

1. Click the Media button in the iWeb toolbar to open the Media panel.

2. Select the Photos tab and find the photo you want to use.

3. Drag the photo from the Media panel onto the placeholder image.

When you drag your image on top of the placeholder, not only is the image replaced, but the reflection is also created on the fly.

> You can get additional templates from http://11mystics.com/blog/. If you have an itch to design your own templates, there is a tutorial available on 11mystics as well at http://11mystics.com/blog/iweb-templates/create-your-own-iweb-templates/.

iWeb blogging

A static site is fine for many instances, but these days most people want to also have a weblog to archive their thoughts online. iWeb lets you create a custom weblog and publish it on the Web (RSS feed included).

To create a blog, click the plus (+) button at the bottom-left corner of the iWeb window (see Figure 14-3).

Figure 14-3.
The plus button lets you add new pages to your iWeb site.

The template pane will drop down again. Select the Blog template. This will create a new subsection of your site in the iWeb Site Organizer. The Blog page gives an introductory paragraph and a listing of your latest entries. Underneath the new blog subcategory is an entries listing and an archive page. The entries listing lets you create a new page for each blog post you write. The archive aggregates all the entries you have written and lists their titles on a single page.

Editing the blog page or a blog entry is the same as editing a static page.

iWeb supports the publishing of comments to your blogs. To add comments, follow these steps:

1. Click the Inspector button in the toolbar.

2. Click the RSS Feed icon in the panel that appears.

3. Check Allow Comments.

4. A warning will appear that tells you how to manage your comments. Click OK.

Adding a podcast

If you have created a podcast using GarageBand or some other method, you can publish it to the Web easily using iWeb. To do this, go to File ➤ New Page and select the Podcast template from the pane that drops down.

The podcast layout is similar to that of your blog: the main podcast page contains a subcategory for entries and an archive page (see Figure 14-4). Also similar to a blog, adding a new entry to your podcast is as simple as creating a new entry.

Figure 14-4.
A podcast, like a blog, contains two subcategories of data: entries and an archive page.

In your new entry, modifying the text and titles is the same as with other aspects of iWeb. To add your actual podcast to iTunes, drag it from the Media Browser, or the Finder, onto the audio droplet in the center of the entry page. This will not only embed the audio in the actual Web page, so it can be played inline, but it will also update the podcast's RSS feed and upload the file to your published site.

You can also submit your podcast directly to iWeb from within GarageBand. From the Share panel in GarageBand, select iWeb as your export option.

Publish to iTunes

In addition to publishing your podcast site and RSS feed to your iWeb site, you can also submit your new podcast directly to iTunes from within iWeb. To submit your podcast, go to File ➤ Submit Podcast to iTunes. A pane will pop down (see Figure 14-5) that has your podcast's title and description already filled in. All you need to do is set your copyright, category, language, and parental advisory information. When you have filled out the results to your liking, click Publish and Submit to send it to iTunes.

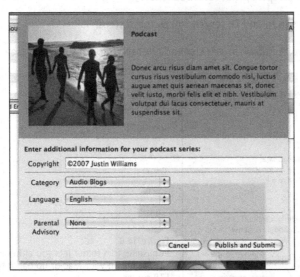

Figure 14-5. You can publish your podcast to iTunes from within iWeb.

14

Publishing your site

iWeb was made with publishing your site to .Mac in mind. Mac is Apple's set of web services that it offers for $99. One of the features it offers is hosting a web page for you to share photos, music, and more.

To publish your iWeb site to .Mac, go to File ➤ Publish All to .Mac. This will upload the entire site to your .Mac account. Before you can upload it, you will receive a warning that you should only upload content that you have content rights for. In other words, don't upload copyrighted material as it risks being removed by Apple.

Uploading can take anywhere from a minute to several minutes depending on how much content you have created for your iWeb site.

Once uploaded, you can then access your page from http://web.mac.com/*username* where *username* is your .Mac username.

Uploading changes

Notice that after you publish your site to .Mac, the Site Organizer's icons turn from red to blue. Blue icons mean that the pages are online. If you make a change to a page or add new pages to your site, their icons will be red to let you know that those changes are not live on the Web. To publish those changes, simply republish the site to .Mac.

FTP publishing

One of the shortcomings of iWeb is its lack of easy support for publishing to a non-.Mac site via FTP or another protocol. To publish via FTP, you will need an FTP client such as Panic's Transmit (http://panic.com/transmit/).

To publish your site to an FTP server, follow these steps:

1. Select File ➤ Publish to a Folder and choose your output folder (see Figure 14-6).

Figure 14-6.
Publishing to a folder lets you either host an iWeb site locally on your Mac or upload it to a third-party FTP server.

2. Launch Transmit and connect to your web server.

3. In Transmit, set Your Stuff to where you published your iWeb site.

4. Drag the iWeb files to the FTP server.

If you don't have an existing web host and just want simple one-click publishing, I'd recommend signing up for a .Mac account and using this web service as your provider. The 10GB of storage you get with a .Mac account is ample to store lots of photos, movies, and podcasts.

Summary

In this chapter, I wrapped up coverage of the iLife suite. I covered how to create a basic web site in iWeb that contains a blog and podcast. The neat thing about iWeb is that it brings the entire suite together by giving you an easy way to publish all the different types of media you created to .Mac or another web server.

In the next chapter, I will be covering Boot Camp, Apple's integrated solution that allows you to run Windows on your Intel-based Mac. If you are running a Mac with a G4 or G5 inside, you can skip the chapter since Boot Camp is a feature for Intel-based machines solely.

14

This chapter covers the following topics:

- What is Boot Camp
- How Boot Camp differs from virtualization
- Setting up Boot Camp
- How to switch between operating systems

Boot Camp is Apple's name for its capability to dual-boot both Mac OS X and Windows on an Intel-based Mac. When you hold down the Option key (Alt) at startup, you are given the option of booting into either Mac OS X or Windows if you have an Intel processor in your Mac.

While Boot Camp was introduced in beta form in the summer of 2006 for Mac OS X Tiger, Apple always said that the final version of Boot Camp would be available with the release of Leopard.

Boot Camp differs from virtualization software like Parallels or VMware in that it does not run on top of Mac OS X. Instead, it is installed on its own hard drive or partition and booted into as the main OS. Boot Camp has the advantage of running at full speed, since it uses all of your Mac's processing power rather than sharing it with Mac OS X.

> *You can learn more about VMware and Parallels by visiting* www.vmware.com/mac/ *and* www.parallels.com/products/desktop/, *respectively.*

Setting up Boot Camp

The first thing you need to use Boot Camp is an Intel-based Macintosh. If you are unsure of what architecture you are running, you can go to the Apple menu and select About This Macintosh. Look in the processor section to see whether your chip was made by Intel, as shown in Figure 15-1.

If you plan on installing Windows on your Mac OS X hard drive, make sure you also have at least 10GB of hard drive space available. You can check your available hard drive space by selecting your hard drive and going to File ➤ Get Info. 10GB is on the low end and covers just the basic Windows installation. If you want to install applications like Office or games, I would recommend preparing to give Boot Camp 20GB of space.

You are going to need a copy of either Windows XP Home, Windows XP Professional (SP2 or above), or any version of Windows Vista. Media Center editions of Windows XP or Vista will not work. Apple doesn't provide the copy of Windows for use with Boot Camp because it isn't in the business of selling Windows. You can easily pick up a copy at your local computer store or online.

Figure 15-1. The About This Mac panel will show what chip architecture you are using.

> *Before you begin, you should back up your Mac. Resizing partitions can be a dangerous task. You should also restart your Mac and leave all your applications closed.*

Partitioning your hard drive

With the requirements out of the way, you can actually go about the process of preparing your Mac for Windows. The first thing you need to do is partition your hard drive. **Partitioning** is the process of dividing a single physical hard drive into several logical drives.

1. To begin, launch the Boot Camp Assistant found in /Applications/Utilities. When it launches, click Continue.

Boot Camp only works with internal hard drives, so you cannot partition any external FireWire or USB2 drives for use with Boot Camp. If you have a Mac Pro, Boot Camp will work with any hard drive that is installed internally.

2. On the Select Task screen of the Boot Camp Assistant, select Create or Remove a Windows Partition. The next screen will let you select the internal hard drive you want to partition.

> *If you have already partitioned your drive, Boot Camp will not be able to work with your drive. It assumes that your drive is still in the same state as when you got your Mac.*

15

3. Select Create a second partition for Windows if you want to split your drive into two partitions. If you have a Mac Pro with a separate drive, you can select Erase disk and create a single partition for Windows if you want to dedicate an entire drive to Windows. Make sure you don't have any important data on the drive you want to erase, because you won't be able to get it back.

4. The partition screen (see Figure 15-2) lets you decide how big you want your Windows and Mac partitions by dragging a divider to the left or right. You can also use the buttons underneath to divide your hard drive in half so each partition is of equal size. Make sure you make your partition at least 10GB. Keep in mind that the Windows drive cannot be larger than 32GB. Boot camp uses the FAT partitioning format, which is unable to recognize a drive larger than 32GB.

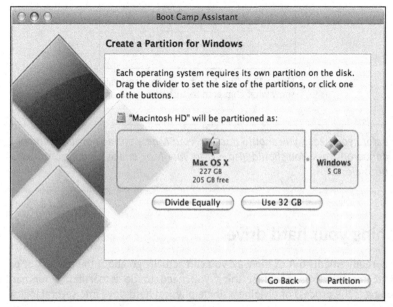

Figure 15-2. The partition screen lets you allocate how much space to give to Mac OS X and Windows XP.

5. Click the Partition button.

Before Intel-based Macs, partitioning your hard drive involved having to erase all the data off your hard drive. With the introduction of Intel-based Macs, Apple introduced a new resizeVolumn subcommand to the Disk Utility. This allows for Mac OS X to partition your hard drive without having to erase your data.

Partitioning can take anywhere from a few minutes to an hour or two depending on the size of your drive.

Installing Windows

With the partitioning process out of the way, proceed with the following steps to install Windows:

1. Insert your Windows disk in your Mac's disk drive.

2. If you have more than one internal disk, select the disk you have partitioned for Windows and then click Continue.

3. Click Start Installation. Your computer will then boot from your Windows CD.

4. Once the Windows installer launches, follow the onscreen instructions. When you get to the partition screen, pay special attention.

> *Do not create or delete a partition, or select any partition other than C:. The other partitions contain your Mac OS X data.*

5. Select partition C:, which should be named BOOTCAMP.

6. The next screen lets you format your BOOTCAMP partition. You can format it as either NTFS or FAT. FAT is more compatible with Mac OS X and lets you read and write data to the drive when you are running Windows. NTFS is read-only, so you cannot write data to the drive from OS X. If you are installing Windows XP, you can choose between NTFS and FAT, but if you are using Vista, you have to stick with NTFS.

7. Once your drive is formatted, use the Windows setup screens to complete your Windows installation.

Installing drivers

After installing Windows, use the Mac OS X Leopard CD to install the drivers to power the hardware inside your Mac. The drivers CD includes software to support the following:

- Video card
- Ethernet or AirPort cards
- Sound
- Bluetooth
- iSight cameras
- Apple keyboards and mice

The drivers disk also installs a Windows Control Panel called Boot Camp that lets you adjust different options related to using your Mac in Windows and selecting your startup disk.

When you insert the Leopard CD, it should launch the setup assistant. If you have AutoRun turned off, double-click the Setup.exe file.

15

As the installer runs, you may notice that a message will appear that says the software you are installing has not passed Windows Logo testing. Click Continue anyway. The software is developed by Apple, but it hasn't gone through the process of getting the software authorized by Microsoft.

Once the setup completes, you will need to restart your Mac so that the hardware will be recognized by Windows.

Switching between systems

Now that you have both Windows XP and Mac OS X installed on your Mac, there are a few ways to switch between the operating systems.

When your Mac boots up, hold down the Option key until disk icons appear on screen (see Figure 15-3).

Figure 15-3. Using your arrow keys, you can switch between your Windows and Mac partitions.

Select the startup disk you want to use using the arrow keys on your keyboard and then press the Enter key to make your selection.

If you want to set Windows to be your default operating system when you boot up, go to the Startup Disk preferences pane in Mac OS X or Startup Disk Control Panel in Windows XP. Select the operating system you want to use by default and then click Restart.

Virtualization with Parallels or VMWare

If you only occasionally need to run Windows or have a single application you need to run, you might not need to install Boot Camp at all. As I touched on earlier, there are two pieces of software that will allow your Intel Mac to run Windows *on top* of Mac OS X (see Figure 15-4). This process is called virtualization, and what it basically does is use software to trick your Mac into thinking it has extra hardware to run an OS on.

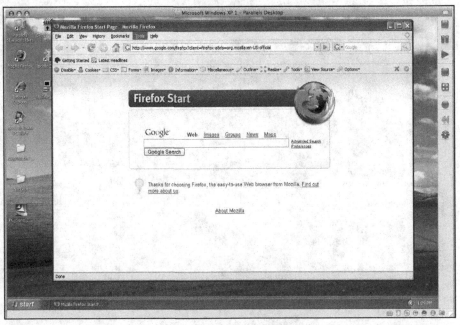

Figure 15-4. Virtualization lets you run another OS in a window on your Mac.

There are two major solutions for running Windows on top of Mac OS X using virtualization technology. The first on the market was Parallels Desktop (www.parallels.com/products/desktop/). Parallels is the easiest to use of the two virtualization platforms for the Mac and has the fastest rate of development presently. The other virtualization solution is from market powerhouse VMware. VMware released Fusion (www.vmware.com/mac/) in the middle of 2007, and it offers a slight speed advantage over Parallels. You should definitely try both applications and decide which one works best for you.

While not nearly as fast as running Boot Camp, virtualization is fast enough to do most things. If you want to play games or run audio or video software, do that in Boot Camp.

Summary

In this chapter, I covered how to use Windows on your Mac with Mac OS X Leopard's Boot Camp feature. You learned how to set up your hard drive to install Windows without losing any of your Mac's files as well as how to install Windows on the Mac. You also learned how to install the necessary drivers to make the Windows experience more usable and how to switch back to Mac OS X Leopard when you are ready.

In the next chapter, I will cover two fun applications that are bundled with Mac OS X: Photo Booth and Front Row.

15

16 FRONT ROW AND PHOTO BOOTH

In this chapter, I will cover the following topics:

- What is Front Row
- Front Row requirements
- Using Front Row
- What is Photo Booth
- Taking photos
- Applying effects
- Sharing your photos

Front Row

Front Row is Apple's media center solution that is now bundled with Mac OS X Leopard. Front Row was introduced in 2005 with the original iMac G5 as a way to view your movies, photos, and DVDs or listen to your iTunes music in a full-screen interface that is controllable with the Apple Remote.

Front Row requirements

Front Row requires that you have at least iLife '06 installed to have support for the iPhoto and iTunes modules of Front Row. Front Row also supports either the Apple Remote or your keyboard for navigating its menus. All Intel Macs, save for the Mac Pro, have shipped with an Apple Remote. The Mac Pro and PowerPC-based Macs do not have the necessary infrared receiver to work with the Apple Remote.

> You can add an IR port to any Mac using a third-party solution such as Twisted Melon's Mantra kit. You can learn more about it at www.twistedmelon.com/.

Using Front Row

To start Front Row, press either the Menu button on your Apple Remote or Cmd+Esc on your keyboard. A chime will play through your Mac's speakers, and your desktop will shrink as the Front Row interface appears on your screen in an elegant transition.

Front Row's interface (see Figure 16-1) mimics that of Apple's AppleTV set-top box. On the left is a large icon for the currently selected menu item. On the right is a listing of the types of media you can work with in Front Row. Front Row has a section for each type of media you can have in iTunes (Movies, TV Shows, Music, and Podcasts) as well as Photos for viewing your iPhoto images. When you drill through the menus, a preview will appear on the left side of the screen as you browse through the files.

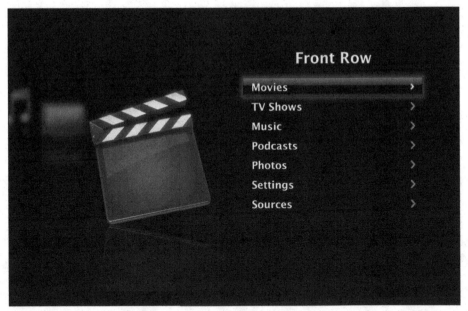

Figure 16-1. The Front Row interface lets you elegantly view multimedia content on your Mac.

Movies

The Movies menu aggregates both the movies stored in your iTunes library as well as the video files it finds in your Movies folder of your home directory. Front Row will display any video that is capable of being played in QuickTime player.

You can also view movie trailers from the Movies menu. The trailers are automatically downloaded from Apple's web site when you want to view them.

TV shows

The TV Shows menu lets you view all the TV shows you have downloaded from the iTunes Store from Front Row. You can browse your TV shows by episode or by the date the show was added to iTunes. When you select an episode, you see a preview of it on your left as well as the episode title, running time, and number.

Music

The Music menu lets you view and listen to your music by the same set of parameters as an iPod: playlist, artist, album, song, genre, composer, or audiobook.

When you are on a song that you want to listen to, the album art and ID3 tag information will appear on the screen as well as the time elapsed and time remaining during the song, just like on an iPod (see Figure 16-2).

Figure 16-2. Playing music via Front Row dedicates half your screen to the album art and the other half to the currently playing song's information.

If you've ever used an iPod, Front Row's Music section should come easy to you.

Podcasts

The Podcasts menu shows you all the podcast episodes, both audio and video, you have inside of iTunes so you can view a listing of them via a full-screen window. When you are navigating your episodes, you will see a preview image, the episode title, and a synopsis on the left of the screen (see Figure 16-3).

Photos

The Photos menu aggregates all the photos and albums in your iPhoto library so that you can display them full screen for your friends and family.

The section has the same organizational structure as your iPhoto library with libraries, smart albums, and regular albums listed. It also has the option for searching for shared libraries on your network.

When you select an album, a slideshow will automatically start with the photos in that album, as shown in Figure 16-4.

Figure 16-3. The Podcasts menu shows you all the audio and video podcasts you have downloaded through iTunes.

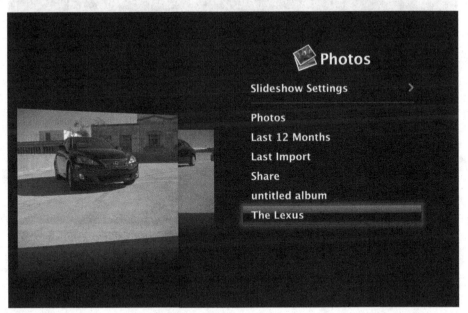

Figure 16-4. You can view slideshows of your iPhoto photographs using Front Row's Photos menu.

Settings

The Settings menu gives you the name of your computer and the version of Front Row you are running, and lets you decide whether to show the screen saver or have interface sound effects when navigating through the interface (see Figure 16-5).

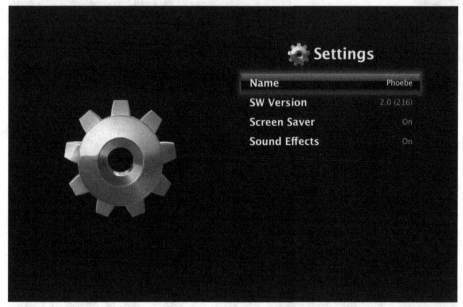

Figure 16-5. The Settings menu lets you adjust whether to play interface sounds or to show the screen saver in Front Row.

Sources

If you have more than one computer running iTunes connected to your network, you can browse their iTunes libraries through Front Row. The Sources menu shows you all the other computers, Mac or PC, that it has found and lets you browse through them (see Figure 16-6).

DVD playback

The DVD menu, which appears at the top of the Front Row interface when you have a DVD inserted into your Mac, lets you play your DVD disks from within Front Row (see Figure 16-7). This is the least complex of all the sections in Front Row. The DVD menu in Front Row gives you the option of resuming the disk from a previous save point if you have played the disk before, starting it from the beginning, ejecting it, or going to the DVD's menu.

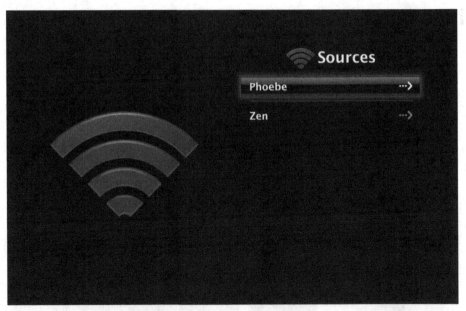

Figure 16-6. The Sources menu lets you see which other computers running iTunes are connected to your home network.

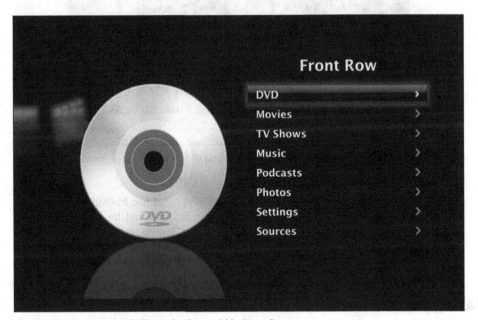

Figure 16-7. You can play DVD movies from within Front Row.

Photo Booth

Photo Booth, shown in Figure 16-8, is a fun application that lets you snap photos of yourself and your friends using an iSight camera. Besides just snapping photos, it lets you apply effects to those photos to distort how you look.

Figure 16-8. Photo Booth lets you snap photos of yourself and your friends using an iSight camera.

Like Front Row, Photo Booth was first bundled with iMacs that had built-in iSight cameras. As more and more Macs included iSight, Apple decided it would be logical to include updated versions of Photo Booth with Mac OS X Leopard. By also bundling it with Leopard, they open the application up to a world of users who have the external FireWire iSight that Apple has sold for the past few years.

Taking photos

Using Front Row is as easy as clicking the red button with the camera icon in the middle of the Photo Booth interface. When you click the button, a 3-second countdown will begin. As the countdown ends, a burst of bright light will appear on your screen to act as a flash, and the snapshot will be taken. Your shot is then added to the photo strip along the bottom of the Photo Booth window (see Figure 16-9).

Figure 16-9. The picture strip at the bottom gives you a preview of all the images you have taken in Photo Booth.

If you want to see your photo again, just click it in the photo view at the bottom. If you find that you don't like the photo, you can click the Delete button below the image.

Besides a single photo, Photo Booth also lets you take four photos in succession and then save them in a single image (see Figure 16-10). To enable this mode, click the middle button on the left side of the Photo Booth window.

Figure 16-10. The new four-shot mode in Photo Booth lets you combine four photos into a single one.

You can also record short videos in Photo Booth by clicking the button with the filmstrip icon on the left side of the interface. With video mode selected, clicking the Snapshot button will give you the same countdown as with photos, but starts recording a video instead (see Figure 16-11). The left side of the screen is replaced with a counter that gives you the length of the video as you are recording it.

Figure 16-11. Photo Booth in Leopard adds support for recording short videos.

Once you are done recording, click the Stop button, and the video will be included in the film strip along the bottom.

Applying effects

While it's fun to just take snapshots of yourself and your friends, it's even more fun to apply effects to those snapshots. Effects let you distort your image or video in colorful and fun ways, as shown in Figure 16-12.

Figure 16-12. The Photo Booth effects view lets you select the effect to apply to your photos.

Effects are separated into four separate views:

- Color distortions such as black and white, sepia, and x-ray
- Filters that mimic how you would look in carnival mirrors
- Backgrounds such as roller coasters and the Eiffel Tower
- Empty backdrops that let you drop in your own photos

To apply one of the filters to your picture, just click it and the effect will appear. Any photos you take with that filter applied will be saved with it.

To remove your filter, just go back to the filters listing and select Normal.

Sharing your photos

Photo Booth integrates with both iPhoto and Apple Mail to allow you to save your photo in your iPhoto library or send it to friends and family via e-mail. When you click one of the images in the picture view along the bottom, the sharing toolbar will appear where the camera button normally is (see Figure 16-13).

Figure 16-13. You can share the photos and movies you shoot in Photo Booth in a variety of ways.

Clicking the Email button will open a new e-mail message that has the photo inside of it. Clicking the iPhoto button will import the selected photo to your iPhoto library.

Besides iPhoto and e-mail support, you can also set a photo to be your iChat buddy picture or Mac OS X account picture.

Summary

In this chapter, I covered two of the unique applications that make the Mac stand out from Windows Vista: Front Row and Photo Booth. You learned what Front Row is and how to use it on your Mac. You also learned how to take fun photos and share them in a variety of ways using the Photo Booth application and your Mac's iSight camera.

In the next chapter, I will cover how to work with user accounts in Mac OS X Leopard.

17 WORKING WITH ACCOUNTS

In this chapter, I will cover the following topics:

- Types of user accounts
- Adding accounts
- Managing user accounts
- Parental controls
- Groups
- Fast user switching

If you live with one or more people, you may have to share your Mac with other members of your household. Each person is different, however, in terms of how he likes his desktop laid out, what applications he wants in his Dock, and what files and music he has. Mac OS X has supported multiple user accounts since its first release and has built on that function-ality with each subsequent release. With Leopard, Apple's biggest addition is that of parental controls, which allow you to limit not only what applications your kids can use, but also what sites they can visit on the Internet and how long they can use the family Mac.

Types of accounts

Mac OS X Leopard supports four different types of user accounts: administrators, standard users, managed with parental controls, and sharing accounts. When you first set up Mac OS X and run it through the setup wizard, you are asked to create an account. By default, that initial account is an administrator account. Administrators have free rein over the sys-tem. They can add and remove applications or users as well as work with protected root folders like the Library or System folders. Administrators also have the ability to run com-mands via Terminal under sudo, which gives temporary root access.

Standard accounts are able to run any application on the system, but aren't able to install or remove them from the Applications folder. They also are restricted to storing files in their home directory rather than anywhere on your Mac.

> *Standard accounts can install certain applications in an* Applications *folder in their home directory, but not all software will work via this method, since many major applications install bits and pieces throughout the system like the root* Library *or* System *folders. The home* Applications *folder is not created by default, but if you create it, OS X will automatically recognize it.*

A managed account has the same characteristics as a standard account, but it is restricted by parental controls set by one of the administrator accounts on your Mac.

The final account type, shared, is new to Leopard. A sharing account does not have a home folder; it is instead used to allow other machines on your network to access shared resources on your Mac such as a shared address book or accessible volume on your machine.

Adding accounts

All your account information is managed in the Accounts preferences pane inside System Preferences. To create a new account, click the plus (+) button at the bottom of the accounts source list. A pane will appear as shown in Figure 17-1.

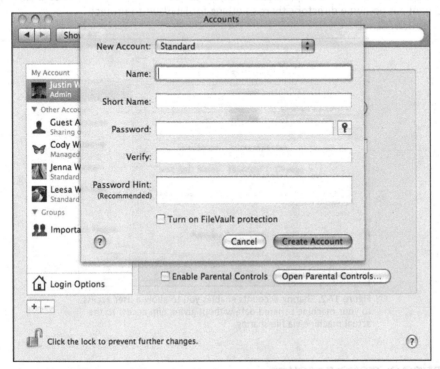

Figure 17-1. Adding an account to your Mac is as easy as filling in a few fields and clicking Create Account.

The first thing you do is select the type of account you want to create. By default, a standard user account is selected, but you can also choose one of the other different account types or a group as well. When adding a user account, you will want to fill in the Name field with the value you would like to appear on the Mac OS X login screen. Usually people enter a person's full name here. The value for Short Name is the actual login the user has for the account. By default, OS X will create the short name from the Name field, but you can modify it to be any value you choose. The Password and Verify fields are self-explanatory.

If you want to make the account an administrator account, make sure you check the appropriate check box. If you would like the account's home directory to be encrypted with Mac OS X's FileVault technology, check that option as well. When you are satisfied with your selections, click Create Account.

Creating a shared account

The process of creating a shared account isn't much different from a standard user account. Once the new account pane appears, change the type to Sharing Only. All the fields that are available for standard accounts will be available, save for allowing the account to enable FileVault protection, as you can see in Figure 17-2. Since a sharing account has no home directory, there's nothing for FileVault to protect.

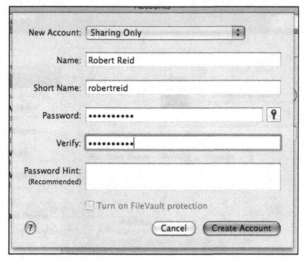

Figure 17-2. Sharing accounts enables you to allow a user access to your machine's shared data without giving him access to the actual machine via file sharing.

Creating a group account

The group account is a new feature in Mac OS X Leopard that allows you to set permissions for a number of accounts from a single point. For example, if you have a folder of files that you'd like a group of family members to have access to, you can create a group that contains all of the family members' user accounts.

> *For more information on working with access control lists, check out* http://maczealots.com/articles/acl/.

Unlike standard and sharing accounts, a group only has one field to fill in, as you can see in Figure 17-3: Name.

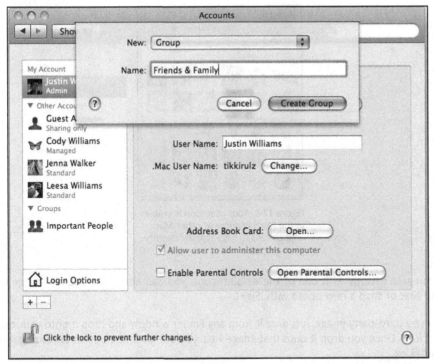

Figure 17-3. Adding a group is the easiest of all account types since there is only one field to fill in!

Managing your accounts

After you have created your accounts, there's some customization you can do to the account such as changing your user icon, changing how users log in to your Mac, or modifying more advanced attributes of your account such as the default Terminal shell.

Modifying the user icon

Apple includes 30 standard user icons, but if you have an external or a built-in iSight camera, you can also take a picture of yourself and use that as your icon. To modify your user icon, select your user account inside the Accounts preferences pane and click the image well that has the current icon you are using. Clicking it will open up a listing of the default icons you can select, as you can see in Figure 17-4.

Figure 17-4. Your user icon is visible in the login window or other Mac applications to help visually identify your account.

If you aren't happy with one of the default icons, you can either use another image on your Mac or snap a new photo with iSight.

To use a third-party image, just drag it from any Finder window and drop it onto your current icon. Once you drop it onto that image well, you are given the option of resizing it to your liking.

If you want to use an iSight image, click your currently selected icon and then choose Edit Picture. A pane will drop down that lets you either edit your currently selected image or take a snapshot with your iSight.

Clicking the iSight icon will open a miniature Photo Booth view with the 3-second countdown and preview window. After you take your photo, you have the option to resize the image to your liking.

Modifying the login window

By default, the Mac OS X login window displays the user icon and full name for each account on your Mac, as you can see in Figure 17-5. Some might consider this a security vulnerability, especially in a protected environment like a corporate office. Apple has a few options you can set to modify the login window.

Figure 17-5. The Mac OS X Leopard login window by default shows all the accounts on your system.

To modify these options, select Login Options from the bottom of the source list. Here you are given several options such as setting up a user whose account automatically logs in when you restart your Mac. Of interest right now, however, is the option that starts with Display login window as. Select Name and Password. Now when you log out, you will only see two text fields: one for the username and one for the password.

You can also disable the Sleep, Restart, and Shutdown buttons on the login window if you want to prevent non–logged in users from restarting the Mac. By default, the option to show those buttons is checked, but disabling it is as easy as unchecking the box.

Parental controls

Parental controls were a part of Mac OS X Tiger, but everything about them was scattered and hard to manage. With Leopard, Apple has moved parental controls into their own preferences pane and even added some enhanced functionality.

Enabling controls

Parental controls can only be enabled on nonadministrator accounts. To enable parental controls for a particular account, select that account in the Accounts preferences pane and check the box next to Enable Parental Controls as in Figure 17-6.

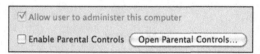

Figure 17-6. Enabling parental controls is as easy as clicking a single check box.

After enabling controls, click the Open Parental Controls button to open the Parental Controls pane. The window looks similar to the Accounts preferences pane in terms of general layout: the source list on the left side gives a listing of accounts that are eligible for parental controls, and the right side has several different tabs with options you can set against each account.

Restricting applications

The System tab on the Parental Controls pane lets you enable the Simple Finder if you have young children using your computer or restrict what applications the user account can access. Enabling this will give you a listing of all the applications currently on your Mac. Apple divides those applications into different categories: iLife, iWork, Internet, Widgets, Other, and Utilities. iLife contains applications bundled in the iLife suite like iMovie, iTunes, and iPhoto. iWork consists of Keynote, Numbers, and Pages. Internet applies to any application that either connects to the Internet such as iChat or Safari or manages your Internet connection such as Internet Connect.

The Widgets category lets you enable or disable certain widgets. The Other category contains all other applications that are found in the /Applications folder on your system. Finally, Utilities contains all the applications in the /Applications/Utilities folder.

Any checked application or widget can be opened by the account. If you look at Figure 17-7, you can see that iTunes and Keynote are disabled.

Besides restricting application access, you can also restrict whether the user can modify your printer information, burn disks, change his password, or modify applications in the Dock.

If you are running a public Mac at a library or some other location, you would most likely want to restrict the machine to only be able to open applications like Safari, but not be able to do much else on the machine.

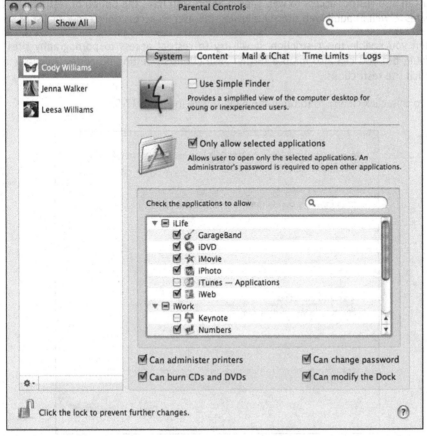

Figure 17-7. Restricting applications and functionality is handled through the System tab in the Parental Controls pane.

Restricting content

If you are dealing with young children, you may want to hide profanity from them. Apple bundles an application with Mac OS X that is a complete dictionary chock full of curse words. If you would rather your children not see that account, you can disable profanity in the dictionary application by enabling the option shown in Figure 17-8, which appears under the Content tab.

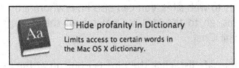

Figure 17-8. You can hide profanity from your young children using Mac OS X's parental controls.

You can also restrict access to web sites in Safari. You have the option of restricting a list of sites as well as adult web sites or allowing the user to access only a specific list of sites.

When you enable this restriction, it will try to restrict access to pornography sites by default, but you can also impose further restrictions by setting up certain bypasses and explicit site restrictions.

To do this, click Configure to open the pane shown in Figure 17-9.

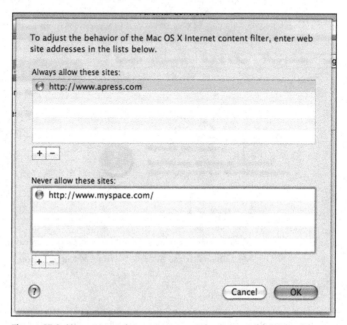

Figure 17-9. You can restrict access to certain sites on the Web with parental controls.

The top table lets you define sites that you want to bypass any filter (the Apress site in this example). Any site included in this list will be given safe passage to the managed account.

To restrict access to a specific site, add it to the bottom table. In this example, access to MySpace is restricted (much to the chagrin of 14-year-olds everywhere).

Safe chatting

Besides restricting access to web sites, you can also limit whom a user can e-mail and chat with in iChat. To do this, go to the Mail & iChat tab of the Parental Controls pane and enable Limit Mail and Limit iChat.

To add an account to the safe list, click the plus (+) button at the bottom of the allowed communications table. A pane will appear as in Figure 17-10 where you can add as many e-mail and chat names as that person has.

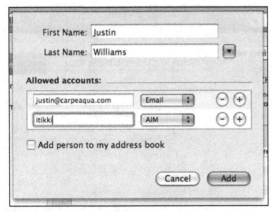

Figure 17-10. You can add a user's e-mail address, AIM screen name, or Jabber screen name to the safe list.

In the instance that the managed user tries to correspond with someone who is not included in the safe communicators list, you can enable a permissions e-mail to be sent to you by putting your e-mail address in the Send permission requests to text field.

Now when the managed user tries to send an e-mail or chat to a person who isn't allowed, you will receive a notification in your inbox that lets you either approve or deny the correspondence.

Time limits

One of my favorite new features in Mac OS X Leopard is the addition of time limits in parental controls. My 14-year-old sister spends hours a day surfing the Web for shoes and fashion rather than doing her homework. With Mac OS X Leopard, I can limit how long she can stay on the computer each night.

There are three different types of time limits you can enable in the Time Limits tab of the Parental Controls pane. You can limit the total amount of time that a user account is logged in to your Mac on weeknights. For example, you can set a user account to be online for 2 hours a night. These limits are in place Monday through Friday (see Figure 17-11).

There are separate limits that you can set for the weekends, since many kids are given different limits for those two days in the week.

Finally, you can limit what hours the user cannot log in to the account. For example, I don't want my sister sitting on MySpace in the middle of the night, so I can restrict her to being logged off of the Mac between 8 p.m. and 6 a.m. during the week and 12 a.m. and 6 a.m. on the weekends.

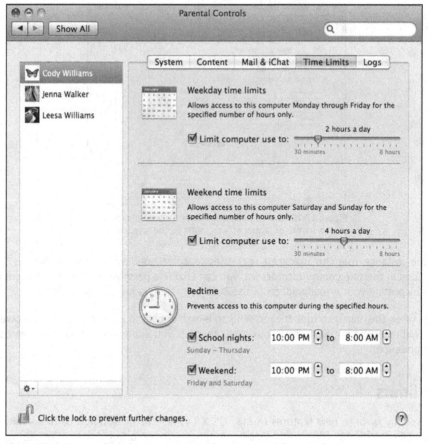

Figure 17-11. You can limit the access managed user accounts have to the computer to certain hours during the day.

Checking the logs

The Logs tab of the Parental Controls pane lets you see what sites your managed users have visited, to whom they have chatted, and what applications they are opening. If you notice that a managed user is visiting a site that you don't want her to see, you can add a restriction for that site by clicking the Restrict button, as shown in Figure 17-12. This also works for applications and iChat buddies.

Figure 17-12. You can check the logs to see what your kids are looking at and further restrict their access if need be.

Copying settings

If you have a general set of restrictions that you want to attach to multiple accounts, you can easily copy those settings between accounts. Click the account that has the settings you would like to copy, click the drop-down menu (with the gear icon) at the bottom of the window, and select Copy Settings (see Figure 17-13).

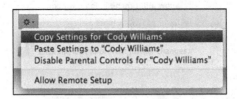

Figure 17-13. You can copy a parental control policy to another account by simply copying it from the first account and pasting it into the other.

Next, select the account you want to apply those settings to and then go back to the drop-down menu and select Paste Settings. Now that account will inherit all the settings applied to the first account. Keep in mind that if you make any changes to one account, they won't be applied to the other without copying and pasting the changes again.

The guest account

The guest account is something that has been a part of Mac OS X for a while, but not until Leopard has Apple actually highlighted it in a user interface. When enabled, the guest account requires no password and lets the user work with the Mac freely. When the account logs out, all data that was created by that user in his home folder is erased from your system, so that he is not able to do any damage to the machine.

To enable the guest account, click the account in the Accounts preferences pane and check Enable Guest Account. It will now be available from the login screen.

User groups

As mentioned earlier, to create a group, click the plus (+) button at the bottom of the account source list and select Group as the account type in the pane that drops down. You can then name the group whatever you want and save it.

All groups you create on your Mac are stored together toward the bottom of the accounts list, as you can see in Figure 17-14. You can add individual user accounts to a group by selecting that group and then putting a check mark by the name of each account that should be a member of that group.

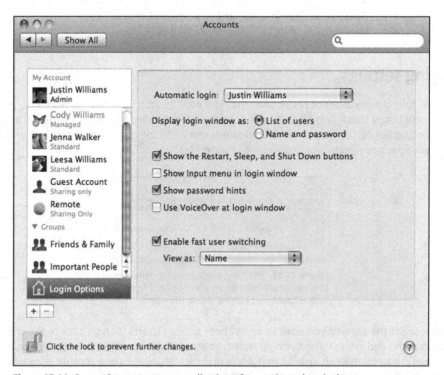

Figure 17-14. Groups let you manage a collection of users through a single proxy.

Fast user switching

If you have multiple people sharing the same Mac and have multiple user accounts, it can be inconvenient to have to log out of your account so someone else can log in. Whenever you log back in, you have to go through the process of opening all your applications and documents again, signing back on to iChat, and opening up your Safari home page. All of this takes time, and if you are like me, you are a bit too impatient to wait. Luckily, Mac OS X has a feature called **fast user switching** that lets you keep multiple accounts signed on in the background while someone else is using the Mac.

To enable fast user switching, go to the Login Options section of the Accounts preferences pane and check Enable fast user switching. You will be prompted with a warning that tells you to let only trusted users use your Mac, as shown in Figure 17-15. Click OK.

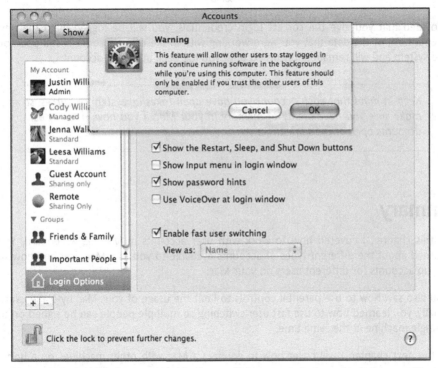

Figure 17-15. Enabling fast user switching lets multiple accounts be logged in at the same time.

With fast user switching enabled, you should now see a new menu next to your Spotlight icon in the upper-right corner of your desktop that has your account name. Clicking that will give you a listing of the other accounts on your system (see Figure 17-16). If you click one of the account names, you will be prompted to log in to that account.

Figure 17-16. Switching users is as easy as clicking another account's name and logging in.

Provided that you give the correct login credentials, you will be logged in to the new account. All of the data that you were working with in the other account is still open on the system and will remain undisturbed until you log back in to that account.

> *Keep in mind that each account you have open takes up system resources, so make sure you have plenty of memory in your Mac if you have a lot of user accounts open at the same time.*

Summary

In this chapter, I covered how to work with user accounts in Mac OS X Leopard. You learned about the different types of accounts available to you as a Mac user and how to set up accounts for different users on your Mac.

You also saw how to use parental controls to limit the usage of your Mac by some users. Finally, you learned how to use fast user switching so multiple people can be signed on to a single machine at the same time.

In the next chapter, I will cover how to connect a Mac with other machines on a home network.

18 NETWORKING YOUR MAC

In this chapter, I will cover the following topics:

- Setting up your network preferences
- Setting your sharing preferences
- Sharing files between two Macs
- Sharing another Mac's screen

While you could keep your Mac off of a network and off the Internet, you will be losing a major part of what makes using a Mac a great experience: the ease of working with other computers on a network and the Internet.

Network preferences

The Network preferences pane (see Figure 18-1) gives you information about all the network connections that are coming out of your Mac. Any Mac that has shipped in the past few years has an Ethernet port, Bluetooth, FireWire, and an AirPort card. Each of these devices can be used to connect your Mac to other Macs on your home network or to the Internet. Usually you will be using the AirPort or Ethernet connection to get online. Bluetooth is good for transferring data between your Mac and your phone. FireWire can be used to do fast transfers between two Macs.

Figure 18-1. The Network preferences pane has been completely redesigned to be more modern and easier to use.

The Network preferences pane has a listing of the network connections on the left in a source list, with the details of the selected connection to the right of it.

In the source list, each connection has a name as well as the connection status: Connected is represented by a green circle, Not Connected by a red circle, and Connection with an Error by a yellow circle. Besides the name of the connection, there is also an icon next to it to help give the user a visual representation as well. True to form, the source list also has a set of buttons at the bottom with a gradient background. Clicking the plus (+) button will let you add another network interface such as a VPN connection if you need it. The minus (–) button lets you remove connections from your active connections. For example, if you don't think you'll ever connect to another Mac via FireWire, you can delete that connection. The drop-down menu (with the gear icon) has other options that let you rename or duplicate connections.

When you have a connection selected such as AirPort or Ethernet, you are given the current IP address, selected network, and other basic information that may be useful for quick tech support. If you need to see more in-depth information like the IPv6 or router address, clicking the Advanced button will drop down a pane with that information.

Setting up your connection

Let's take a look at how you'd set up a connection via AirPort or through Ethernet.

AirPort

Mac OS X Leopard makes joining a new wireless network as easy as a few button clicks.

If you are coming from a Windows XP environment, you know that getting on a wireless network isn't necessarily an easy or intuitive task. You open the connection manager and double-click the network you want to join. If the network is password protected, you need to enter the hex equivalent of the password rather than straight text.

Not on the Mac.

To join a wireless network in Mac OS X, open your Network preferences pane and select AirPort. The Network Name pull-down menu will show all of the available wireless networks (see Figure 18-2).

Figure 18-2. AirPort will try to find all the available wireless networks within range of your Mac.

> *When you open your Mac, it will automatically try to join open networks by default.*

When you select your network, you may also need to enter a password to pass the wireless security credentials. Enter the plain text password and then click Join.

No hex passwords, no weird connection managers. Take that, Windows!

Ethernet

Connecting to a network via Ethernet is even easier than with AirPort. If you are connected to a network that is using a DHCP server, you should automatically get an IP address and be online.

If you need to set your IP information manually, change the Configure drop-down option to Manually and enter the necessary information as in Figure 18-3. You can most likely get this from your system administrator if you aren't sure of it.

> *Obviously you should have your Ethernet cable plugged into your Mac as well.*

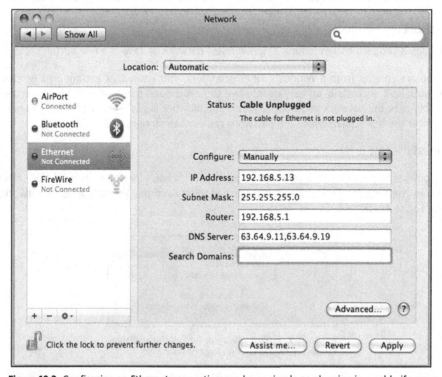

Figure 18-3. Configuring an Ethernet connection can be as simple as plugging in a cable if you are using DHCP for IP address allocation. If you're not, you will need to enter your IP information manually.

Obviously, you should have your Ethernet cable plugged into your Mac as well.

When you have all of your IP information entered correctly, click Apply to make your settings active.

Prioritizing connections

If you're like me and have a Mac laptop that you carry with you, you may find you want to be connected via AirPort at times and via Ethernet at others. For example, at home I am connected to our local network via AirPort, but at the office I plug my laptop in via Ethernet. I like having Ethernet at the office since I am usually just sitting at my desk, and having the faster connection between my two machines lets me transfer files more quickly.

Mac OS X lets you prioritize which connection the system will use to get you on the network based on your personal preferences. To do this, click the drop-down menu (with the gear icon) at the bottom of the source list and select Set Service Order (see Figure 18-4).

Figure 18-4. Setting your service order lets you prioritize your network connections.

A pane will drop down that lets you drag your connections around to an order you prefer. Connections at the top of the list take priority over those lower on the list.

I tend to put FireWire at the top of my connection list with Ethernet and AirPort following. I like having FireWire at the top because if I connect two Macs via it, I am transferring at a much faster speed than regular Ethernet. If I disconnect my FireWire cable, it will default back to Ethernet.

Managing locations

If you are a mobile warrior, you may also have different network settings between two different places. For example, if you are at a coffee house, you may want to disable your Bluetooth connection, since it won't necessarily be useful.

To set up multiple locations, look at the Location drop-down menu toward the top of the Network preferences pane (see Figure 18-5).

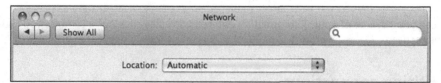

Figure 18-5. The Location drop-down menu lets you switch between different network settings on your Mac.

To create a new location, click the menu and select Edit Locations. A pane will appear that lets you see your current locations and add a new one. As you can see in Figure 18-6, the location manager has a drop-down menu (sporting a gear icon) that lets you manage your locations. Click it and select Duplicate Location to create a copy of your current location.

Figure 18-6. The location manager displays your locations and lets you add new ones.

Select your newly created location, and click the Done button to close the pane. You can now add and remove network connections as necessary or use different IP information. The changes will only be reflected in this specific location profile. Once you are done making your changes, click the Apply button.

Once you have configured your locations to your liking, you can easily switch between them from the Apple menu by selecting Location (see Figure 18-7). Switching between the locations is done automatically.

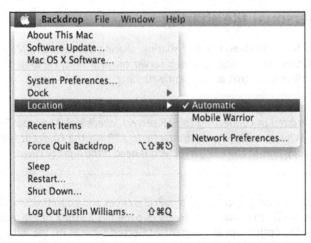

Figure 18-7. Switching locations can be done from the Apple menu.

18

Sharing preferences

If you have more than one Mac (or PC) on your network, you will most likely want to share files between the two systems. Mac OS X is the most network-friendly operating system available today. It supports far more connection methods than other operating systems like Windows. Let's look at some of the major ones:

- **Apple File Protocol (AFP)**: AFP is the default sharing method used to transfer files between two Macs.

- **Server Message Block (SMB)**: SMB is the network protocol used by Microsoft Windows to share files between two machines.

- **File Transfer Protocol/Secure File Transfer Protocol (FTP/SFTP)**: FTP lets you transfer files to any machine that has an FTP server running. SFTP is the same as FTP, but behind a more secure connection.

- **Secure Shell (SSH)**: SSH is the successor to Telnet in that it allows a remote connection to a machine via command line, but with a more secure connection.

- **Bonjour (formerly Rendezvous)**: Bonjour is Apple's technology that lets you search out other computers on your local network instantly and get information about them. Bonjour is used to share bookmarks, address cards, and more.

Setting up personal file sharing

This section will focus on three types of sharing: sharing between two Macs, sharing with Windows computers, and setting up a web server on your Mac. Personal sharing lets you share between other Macs that are presently running.

> *If you are interested in connecting to FTP servers, check out Appendix B for a list of great clients. While you can connect directly to FTP via the Finder, it is read-only. If you want to copy files to the FTP server, you'll need a third-party client.*

To enable personal sharing, open up System Preferences and go to the Sharing preferences pane (see Figure 18-8). The Sharing preferences pane has a listing of the available services on the right and the options for the currently selected services on the left.

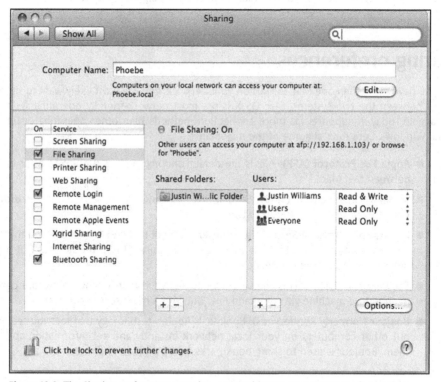

Figure 18-8. The Sharing preferences pane lets you enable access to your Mac from other machines on your home network.

Enabling personal sharing is as simple as checking the box next to Personal File Sharing. The only other option you may want to set is renaming your machine's sharing name from the default *Your Name*'s Computer. You can do this by modifying the value in the Computer Name text field at the top of the Sharing preferences pane. The value you enter here is what will be seen in the Mac OS X network browser.

If you want to offer more fine-grained permissions, you can restrict which users have what sort of file sharing access at the bottom of the File Sharing options. For example, if you wanted to allow other members of your family with their own user accounts access to only your Music folder, you could set a permission on it to allow it.

1. Click the plus (+) button underneath Shared Folders to open a folder selection window.

2. Select the Music folder.

3. By default you will have access to the folder, and everyone else will have no access. Click the plus (+) button underneath Users to select a user or group. You have the option of allowing the user to only copy files (Read Only), copy and write files to the folder (Read & Write), or only copy files, but not be able to see what else is in there (Drop Box).

4. Set the access on the group or user as you desire (see Figure 18-9).

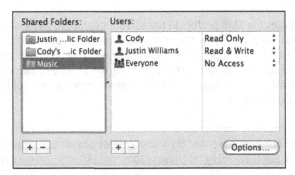

Figure 18-9. You can set permissions on single folders so other users on your Mac can access them without giving them full access to your home folder.

Setting up Windows sharing

If you have Windows machines on your network that you would like to have access to your Mac, you will need to set up SMB sharing. You can enable this by clicking the Options button in the lower-left corner of the File Sharing options to open the pane shown in Figure 18-10. Check Share files and folders using SMB.

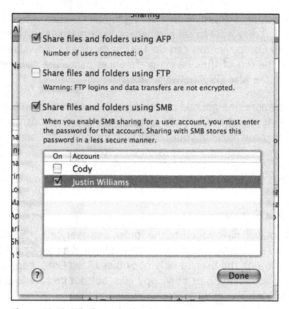

Figure 18-10. Windows sharing is a two-step process: enabling sharing and then enabling specific accounts.

Windows sharing uses the SMB protocol I talked about earlier to allow access to your Mac, and the passwords used are less secure than the passwords your Mac uses by default. If you enable an account to support Windows sharing, your account password will be rehashed using the less secure SMB system. Enabling this on one or two accounts may not necessarily be harmful to you, but you can understand why Apple wouldn't want to have this enabled on a global basis.

> For more information on how Mac OS X implements password authentication, check out www.dribin.org/dave/blog/archives/2006/04/28/os_x_passwords_2/.

To enable specific accounts for SMB sharing, click the check box next to the account. You will be asked to enter the password for that account so that OS X can rehash the password. Once you have enabled all of your accounts, click Done. You should now be able to see your Mac from any Windows PC on your network.

Setting up a web server

If you're like me, one of your favorite features of Mac OS X is that it comes bundled with the Apache web server, so building web sites locally is a cinch. Apache is the most widely used web server on the Internet. To enable Apache, go to the Sharing preferences pane and check Personal Web Sharing. This will turn on the web server in the background.

To test this out, open up Safari and go to http://localhost/. You should get a screen similar to Figure 18-11.

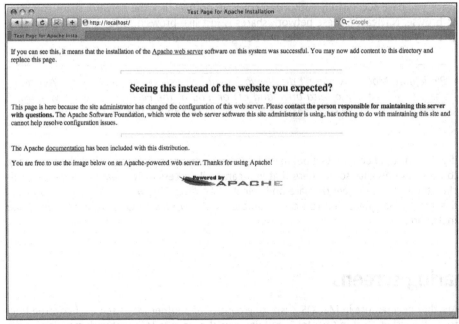

Figure 18-11. When enabled, you can visit http://localhost to see your web server.

The page you are seeing is located in /Library/WebServer/Documents. Any file you store there is accessible via the local web server.

Besides the global web server, you can also access user account–specific web sites by visiting http://localhost/~*username*, where *username* is the short name for each account. The files for these URLs are stored in the Public directory in your home folder.

Sharing between two Macs or PCs

I have discussed the major types of file sharing available on Mac OS X, but I have yet to actually show you how to set up a share between two machines. Let's do that now.

On the Mac you want to mount the shared disk on, open a Finder window and look for the available machines under the Shared portion of the sidebar as in Figure 18-12. Click the machine you want to access, and you will see a listing of the available folders you can mount via the network.

When you select the machine you want to join, you will automatically be connected via the Guest account I talked about in Chapter 17. If you want to access the Mac using another account you have access to on that machine, click the Connect As button in the upper-right corner. If you are connecting to a Windows share, you will also have the option of specifying the Windows domain you are connecting to.

Figure 18-12.
The Go menu in the Finder gives you quick access to the major folders on your Mac.

Once you have successfully authorized yourself, double-click the network share you want to browse. Navigating these network shares is just like browsing your own Mac's folders. The only difference is that the files are being transferred over the network.

> By default, Mac OS X doesn't display your connected shares on the desktop. You can show them just like a hard drive and CD or iPod in the Finder Preferences window. Under General, make sure the Connected servers option is checked.

If you want to keep a quick bookmark to a share you are commonly using, the best thing to do is save an alias somewhere that you can easily access it. To create an alias, Control-click the mounted network share and select Make Alias. This will create an alias on your desktop to that share that you can double-click at any time to launch the connection to that share.

Sharing screens

Another new feature in Mac OS X is taking control of another Mac's screen. I covered how to do this using iChat in Chapter 5, but you can also do it to local network machines using the Finder's network browser. If you are able to share the screen, you will see a Share Screen button next to the Connect As button discussed in the previous section (see Figure 18-13).

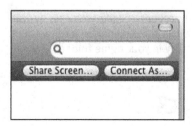

Figure 18-13.
Screen sharing lets you control the mouse and keyboard on another Mac connected to your network.

Clicking Share Screen will open the Screen Sharing application, which asks you to log in to the other Mac. Once you properly authenticate, a window will appear that displays the other Mac's desktop (see Figure 18-14). You can use your mouse and keyboard inside the other user's Mac just as if it were your own.

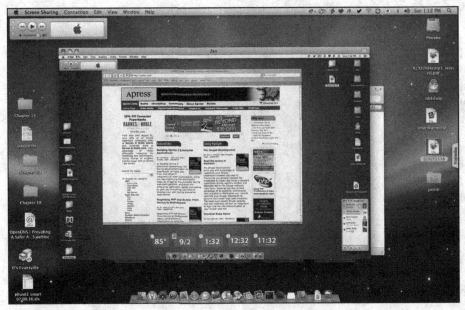

Figure 18-14. When you control another Mac via screen sharing, you can perform the same functions on the other machine as you could if you were sitting in front of it.

When you are finished sharing the screen, just close the window, and the session will end.

Summary

In this chapter, I covered networking options available in Mac OS X. You learned how to set up your Mac to connect to networks via the Network preferences pane. You also created different locations so you could store different network profiles.

You learned about sharing files and folders with other machines using personal and window file sharing. You also saw how to share web pages using the built-in Apache web server. Finally, you saw how to take control of another Mac's screen using the new Screen Sharing application built into Mac OS X Leopard.

In the next chapter, I will cover some best practices for securing your Mac.

19 MAC SECURITY

☑ Enable Firewall Logging
Provides information about firewall activ
sources, blocked destinations, and block

☐ Enable Stealth Mode
Ensures that any uninvited traffic receive
acknowledgement that your computer e:

FileVault secures your hom
encrypts and decrypts you

WARNING:Your files will be enc
password and you don't know t

A master password is **set** f
This is a "safety net" password.
FileVault account on this comp

FileVault protection is **off** f
Turning on FileVault may take a

☑ Require password to wake this com

For all accounts on this computer:
☑ Disable automatic login
☐ Require password to unlock eacl
☐ Log out after 60 ⬍ minutes
☑ Use secure virtual memory

☐ Disable remote control infrared
This computer will work with any avai
remote.

In this chapter, I will cover the following topics:

- How Mac security and Windows security differ
- Setting up a firewall
- Using FileVault
- Commonsense security practices

Mac security vs. Windows security

Mac OS X and Windows Vista share many similarities in how they implement their security model. Both operating systems employ an accounts-based security model. As I mentioned in Chapter 17, giving each user his own account not only is a great way to allow each person using your computer to keep his own files private, but also lets you secure your machine with account-based restrictions. The permissions let you restrict users' data and access to certain parts of the system by the rights associated with their unique user accounts.

The major difference in how the two systems implement their accounts is that Vista offers a more annoying implementation. Both Vista and Leopard prompt the user, even if she is an administrator, for an additional logon and confirmation when the user, or a program she is running, attempts to do something that requires elevated privileges. For example, whenever you update an application like iTunes through Apple's Software Update, you must authenticate with an administrator, or root, account.

Mac OS X uses **sudo**, a framework that runs behind the scenes in Mac OS X's Unix back end, to implement its root access privileges. In its default configuration, sudo authenticates your account for a period of time, during which you can run any privileged task repeatedly without having to provide your login and password again. Windows Vista, on the other hand, will nag you for each and every action it wants to perform.

Which you prefer depends on whether you are concerned more with security or convenience. Having to authenticate only once makes Mac OS X a more pleasurable experience, but security experts will argue that Vista's model is more secure since you have to explicitly allow each action.

> Apple has parodied Vista's security model with its "Security" ad for the Get a Mac campaign. You can watch it at www.apple.com/getamac/ads/.

For someone coming to the Mac for the first time from Windows, it might seem odd to not immediately install software like spyware removers and antivirus software. While these applications are available for the Mac, many users don't feel the need to use them because Mac OS X is not as large of a target as Windows. With Apple only having around 4–5% of the computer market share worldwide, malware creators aren't likely to target the operating system.

Don't infer that Mac OS X is a more secure environment based on this fact. It's not. The debate on the security of Windows vs. Mac OS X will continue for many years to come. However, I do believe that if you follow the steps outlined in this chapter, you won't need to install that antivirus software or spyware removal tool.

Setting up the Mac OS X firewall

Mac OS X includes a powerful built-in firewall that allows you to filter incoming network traffic into your Mac. This is useful, for example, if you don't want to allow remote computers around the world to connect to your Mac via various network protocols such as SSH, FTP, or Windows file sharing. When you block a connection from one of these services, remote computers won't know that you have the services enabled. When they try to connect to them, the firewall will not allow them to pass through.

The Mac OS X firewall can be configured in the Security preferences pane shown in Figure 19-1 (accessed by clicking the Security tab in the System Preferences application).

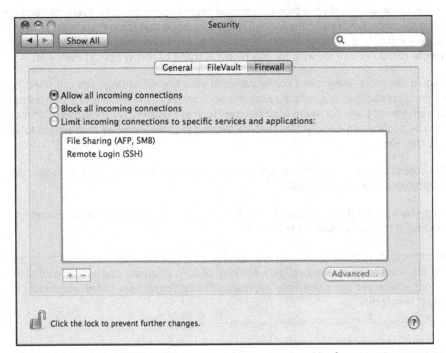

Figure 19-1. The Mac OS X firewall lets you restrict access to your Mac from remote computers around the world.

By default, the firewall does not restrict any sort of traffic. As you can see in Figure 19-1, it also predefines exceptions for you based on sharing options you have enabled in the Sharing preferences pane. If you want to block all traffic from being able to access your machine, select Block all incoming connections. This will prevent any access to your machine from a remote connection.

If you click the Advanced button, you have the option of enabling or disabling logging of your firewall's activity and whether or not to enable stealth mode (see Figure 19-2). If you want to see your firewall in action, set it to block all incoming connections, wait a few minutes, and then click the Open Log button. You will see various attempts to access your Mac by remote computers.

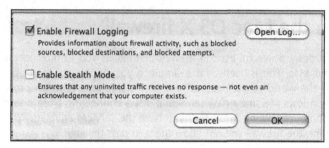

Figure 19-2. The Advanced options for the Mac OS X firewall let you configure logging and whether or not to enable stealth mode.

Stealth mode will modify the type of response your machine sends to a remote computer trying to connect. Normally, the firewall will just respond that the remote machine cannot access the machine. With stealth mode enabled, the response will be modified to trick the remote computer into thinking the machine it is trying to access doesn't even exist.

If you'd like more fine-grained configuration of your firewall settings, you can select Limit incoming connections to specific services and applications in the Security preferences pane. This lets you not only configure what services (such as SSH and FTP) are allowed for access, but also applications on your Mac that are allowed to make incoming connections to your Mac (see Figure 19-3).

The applications and services you specify here will be able to pass through to your Mac, but anything else will be denied.

Once you have finished configuring your firewall, there is nothing else to do. Everything is handled in the background by Mac OS X.

If you want to be able to configure blocking of both incoming and outgoing connections, check out the third-party application Little Snitch (www.obdev.at/products/littlesnitch/).

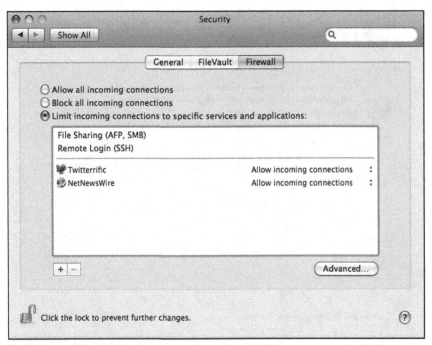

Figure 19-3. If you want to tweak your firewall settings, Mac OS X lets you adjust which services and applications are allowed to pass through.

Using FileVault

If you are paranoid about your data being compromised if you were to lose your laptop, you can use Apple's FileVault technology to encrypt your home directory. FileVault works by creating an encrypted disk image of your home folder. FileVault uses 128-bit encryption keys to ensure that your data is safe from anyone who tries to crack your password.

With FileVault enabled, your home directory will be unmounted and locked down whenever you log out of your Mac. While this makes your computer safer, it does prevent you from using certain sharing features in Mac OS X. For example, since your home directory is an encrypted disk image, other users on the machine and your network won't be able to see your network shares. FileVault may also slow the performance of your machine since it is encrypting and decrypting data on the fly. Another downside to FileVault is that it cannot use Time Machine or any other backup application to browse and restore individual files in your home directory. If this is something important to you, you may be better off not enabling FileVault.

If you decide that, despite the trade-offs, FileVault is worth enabling, doing so is incredibly easy. In the Security preferences pane, go to the FileVault tab (see Figure 19-4).

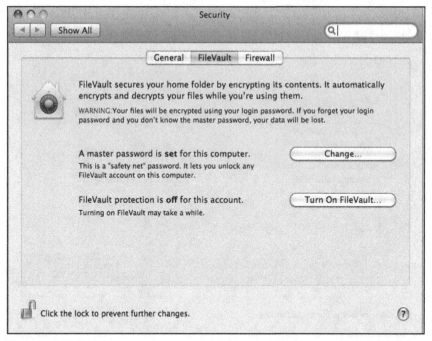

Figure 19-4. FileVault lets you encrypt the contents of your home directory so others don't have access to it if your machine is stolen or compromised.

The FileVault screen has two buttons. The first, Change, lets you set the master password for your computer. The master password is used to decrypt a FileVault directory if you happen to forget your user account's login and password. Make sure you set the master password to something you will remember. If you forget both the user's password and the master password, you are out of luck when it comes to getting your data back.

The second option is to turn FileVault on. Clicking Turn On FileVault starts the process of encrypting your home directory, which can take anywhere from a few minutes to several hours depending on how much data you have stored. During the encryption process, you will be asked to give your user account's password.

Once you have FileVault enabled, you shouldn't notice any difference in your workflow, as everything is handled by Mac OS X behind the scenes.

Common-sense security

Beyond setting up the Mac OS X firewall or using FileVault to encrypt your home directory, you can do some common-sense things to protect yourself while using your Mac. These are all things I incorporate in my daily computing usage, and I have never run into an issue with viruses or malware on my machine.

Password-protect your machine when you are away

If you are in a public environment with your Mac, you can protect your machine when you step away from your desk by prompting for a password to be entered before unlocking the screensaver. To do this, follow these steps:

1. Open System Preferences and go to the Security tab.

2. Check Require password to wake this computer from sleep or screen saver (see Figure 19-5).

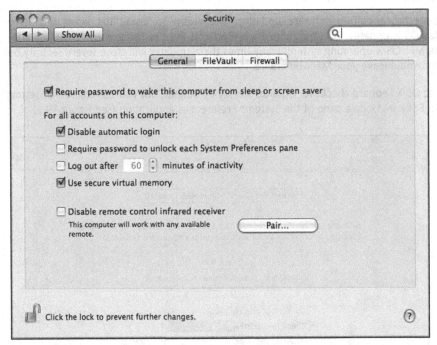

Figure 19-5. Requiring a password to wake from sleep or a screen saver helps protect your Mac from passersby having access to your machine.

3. A pane will pop up that asks if you want to disable automatic login as well. Click Yes.

By disabling automatic login, you are also thwarting another method of attack by requiring that a user log in to his account after your Mac is restarted.

Use strong passwords

As I outlined before, to do any major activity to your Mac, you need to share your password. One of the wisest things you can do is make that password hard to guess should anyone gain physical access to your Mac. Your password should be a mix of letters, numbers, and symbols and be at least eight characters.

Limit users with administrator access

If you have other people using your Mac such as your children, think about whether they need to be administrators on the machine. Administrator accounts have the ability to cause havoc because they can install and remove applications, modify the System directory, and even remove other people's user accounts. If you want someone to only be able to use the applications already on your Mac, just set her up with a standard account.

Keep your Mac up to date

Apple has a built-in software updating mechanism to install the latest security and Mac OS X updates. Do not ignore these updates! Besides fixing issues that may arise in the Mac OS X operating system, many times these updates will close severe security holes that would leave your Mac vulnerable.

Mac OS X Leopard checks for updates weekly by default, but you can adjust that setting in the Software Update pane of the Systems Preferences application (see Figure 19-6).

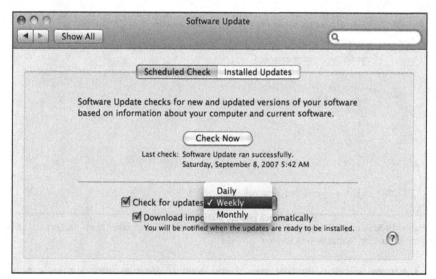

Figure 19-6. Mac OS X checks for updates weekly, but you can check daily or monthly if you prefer.

Think before you click

More important than anything else I have covered in this chapter is the following simple tip: think before you click. Before you click a link you receive in an e-mail or iChat message, think to yourself whether it is a legitimate source. Many times you will receive spam that pretends to be from your bank or some other source asking you to provide personal information such as bank account numbers after you click a link in the e-mail. If this seems suspicious, *don't click it*.

Using discretion and better judgment when working on the Internet is the best thing you can do to protect yourself.

Summary

In this chapter, I covered the security model differences between Windows Vista and Mac OS X Leopard. You learned how to enable the Mac OS X firewall to limit the types of network traffic that can be sent to your Mac. You also saw how to encrypt your home directory using Apple's FileVault technology. Finally, I gave you some common-sense security practices you should adopt so that you have a safe computing environment.

In the next chapter, I will cover Mac OS X's Unix underpinnings and what they mean to you as a Mac user.

19

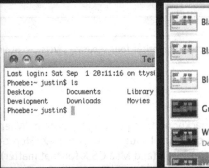
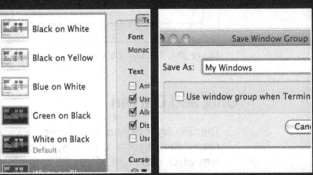

In this chapter, I will cover the following topics:

- The building blocks of OS X
- The Mac OS X shell

The four layers of the Mac OS X architecture

When most people boot up and use their Mac, they probably don't think about how the system actually works. They just realize they are using a beautiful and intuitive user interface that makes working with computers an enjoyable experience. So, if you don't really care what happens behind the scenes, then you don't have to read this chapter.

More seasoned computer professionals, however, are interested in how things work under the hood. Geeks like to tweak and understand every aspect of the system, and Mac OS X is incredibly open about that functionality. As you can see in Figure 20-1, there are four layers to the Mac OS X system architecture. Let's take a look at each one of them here.

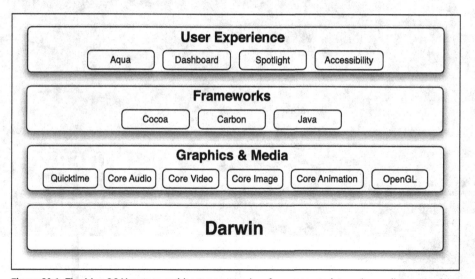

Figure 20-1. The Mac OS X system architecture comprises four separate layers (according to Apple).

Unix and Darwin

The Unix layer of Mac OS X is the backbone that powers the system. When Apple purchased NeXT back in the 1990s, the company brought along its NeXTStep operating system, which is the root of Mac OS X. NeXTStep (and Mac OS X for that matter) is built on a customized version of BSD called **Darwin**. BSD, which stands for Berkeley Software Distribution, is the name for the branch of Unix that Mac OS X uses. BSD has been around since the 1970s and is still used and developed to this day. There are several different variations of BSD, and Apple chose to use FreeBSD.

> *You have probably heard of another implementation of Unix called Linux.*

Apple took the BSD core, tweaked and modified it to its tastes, and then put it at the core of Mac OS X. Being that BSD is an open source project, Apple has also made sure to share its changes in the Darwin project (http://developer.apple.com/opensource/). Darwin is freely available from Apple's web site to download and install on your machine if you are looking for a BSD back end to run on an Intel or a PowerPC machine. Keep in mind, though, that it is only the Unix layer of Mac OS X. You won't have any of the other niceties of the OS like Aqua, nor will you be able to run Mac applications since it's missing the OS X frameworks.

64-bit support

In Mac OS X Tiger, Apple touted its support for 64-bit CPUs like those in the G5 and, more recently, the Intel Xeon that powers the Mac Pro. 64-bit processors offer major benefits to the Mac platform. Besides the faster computational speed, they also break through the RAM barrier and allow for 8GB of RAM in a G5, and up to 16GB in a Mac Pro. RAM is something that people in video production and science fields crave, so 64-bit support was a big bonus for the Mac. By having more RAM, developers can program against a large data set such as the human genome even more easily because they may be able to bring in the entire data set at once instead of portions at a time.

Unfortunately, Tiger's 64-bit support was only for command-line Unix applications. Desktop applications and even the Mac system itself were not 64-bit optimized. With Leopard, however, the entire Mac OS X stack supports 64-bit CPUs. From the Darwin core, all the way up to the Aqua interface, everything is optimized to take advantage of a 64-bit CPU when necessary.

> *One common misconception with 64-bit CPUs is that they are faster for anything and everything. This isn't necessarily true. If you are computing a large data set, it is defi-nitely a benefit to be using 64-bit CPUs because they can crunch that data set far faster. If you are just chatting in iChat, you probably won't notice much of a benefit from a 64-bit CPU vs. a 32-bit CPU.*

Graphics and media

The graphics and media layer of Mac OS X defines all the media APIs and frameworks that are supported by Mac OS X. An API is a set of instructions that programmers can use to hook into technology in their own programs. Combined, the graphics layer of Mac OS X is referred to as Quartz, and it includes the following:

- **OpenGL**: OpenGL is a standard that defines a set of common API calls for building 3D applications. OpenGL is not specific to the Mac, but is instead a standard that is implemented across multiple platforms such as Windows and Linux.

20

- **QuickTime**: QuickTime is Apple's in-house media framework for playing and encoding different types of media.

- **Core Audio**: Core Audio allows programmers to interface with a Mac's sound card easily without having to write their own sound-processing code. Beyond basic sound output, Core Audio also lets programmers add effects in real time to the outputted audio. For example, it's relatively easy to add reverb or equalize an audio stream with Core Audio.

- **Core Image**: Core Image was introduced in Mac OS X Tiger and is the visual counterpart to Core Audio. Using Core Image, programmers can apply several different filters to an image in real time, such as sharpening or converting a photo to sepia.

- **Core Video**: Core Video is a sibling to Core Image and allows you to apply Core Image filters to a video stream.

- **Core Animation**: Core Animation makes it incredibly easy for developers to implement animation and fade effects into their application's user interface.

Frameworks

The frameworks layer defines the different application programming frameworks that can be used by Mac developers.

- **Cocoa**: Cocoa is the preferred development environment for building Mac applications. It is based on the Objective-C language. Besides Objective-C, Leopard also includes a Python and Ruby bridge to allow developers to build Cocoa applications using those languages.

- **Carbon**: Carbon is a set of C APIs developed as an easy way to port classic applications from Mac OS 9 to Mac OS X.

- **Java**: Java is the often forgotten development environment for Mac OS X. While Apple deprecated the Java-Cocoa bridge with Leopard, you can still run Java-native applications such as Azureus or Limewire.

Aqua and the user experience

Part of the user experience layer, Aqua is the public face of Mac OS X. The Aqua interface is rendered using Apple's Quartz rendering technology. Quartz's powerful rendering capabilities are what make the Mac interface look so beautiful.

The Mac OS X shell

The BSD core is hidden from the Finder, but you can access it via the Mac OS X Terminal application. The Terminal is one of the applications stored in the /Applications/Utilities folder. Apple hides the core by default, because it realizes that most users aren't interested in seeing that data on their screen—it is cryptic unless you really understand a Unix system. It could be catastrophic if someone ignorantly deleted the /etc or /var folder from his system.

By using the Terminal application, you are able to see and work with these files (and potentially delete them!).

If it's so dangerous to mess with this stuff, why even bother? Power. The most difficult things to grasp often confer the most power. If you're a software developer, for example, being able to navigate the inner workings of Mac OS X can give you a greater understanding of how your application runs at a detailed level.

> *Here's something interesting to think about: your Mac running OS X is running the same core as most of the servers on the Internet today. BSD and Unix are seen as rock-solid cores for running mission-critical applications in both the private and public sector. Apple building its next-generation operating system on that core speaks volumes for its power and stability.*

20

Terminal basics

Before I cover the more advanced aspects of Terminal, let's open it up and go over the basic interface. As mentioned previously, Terminal is located in /Applications/Utilities. When you first open it, you will see a window similar to Figure 20-2.

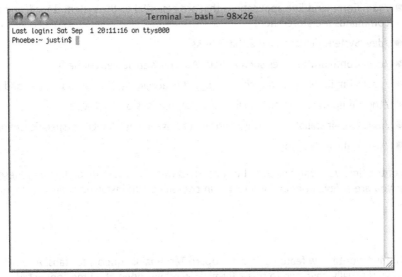

Figure 20-2. The default Mac OS X shell doesn't look like much, but it provides an interface to a wealth of power.

The Terminal window is a basic Aqua window with a shell prompt on it. The prompt shows you where you are in the hierarchy, and you can enter commands at the prompt. From this you can navigate around your local system. By default, when you open a Terminal window, you are placed in your home directory. To prove this, type in pwd and press Return. You should see an output similar to /Users/*shortname*.

If you have ever used Windows or DOS, this is similar to the `C:\` *command prompt.*

To get a listing of the files and folders in the directory you are currently in, type ls and press Return. You should see output similar to what is shown in Figure 20-3.

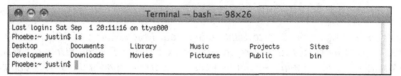

Figure 20-3. The ls command gives you a listing of the files and folders in the directory you are currently in.

To navigate to another folder, you can use the cd command. For example, to switch to your Desktop folder, type cd Desktop. Now if you get a listing of the files, it will contain the files that are located in your home directory.

Let's get out of the home directory and get a view of the entire system. To do this, type cd / and press Return. / is the root directory of your Mac. If you get a listing (ls) of the folders and files, you will see a lot of cryptic folders. The following list briefly defines them:

- /bin: Command-line applications that are essential to the system. ls, cd, and other commands are stored here.
- /dev: System devices such as hard disks.
- /etc: Configuration files such as your Apache web server config files.
- /sbin: Similar to /bin, but containing utility applications such as launchd and ping.
- /tmp: Temporary files and sockets used by services on your Mac.
- /usr: User-installable software and utilities as well as Mac OS X–specific utilities.
- /var: Data such as logs.

Most of the time you won't need to be concerned with the structure and data in these files unless you are a developer and interested in compiling and installing your own software.

Tabs

One of my favorite new features of the Leopard Terminal is support for tabs. As a software developer, I usually have two to three Terminal windows open at a time connected to multiple servers or local applications. Now, instead of having three different windows cluttering my desktop, I can keep them all inside a single Terminal window container, much like browsing multiple web sites via Safari tabs.

To open a new tab in Terminal, go to the Shell menu and select New Tab. A tab bar will drop down below the title bar of the Terminal window as shown in Figure 20-4.

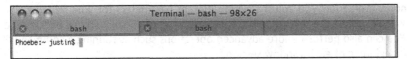

Figure 20-4. Tab support in Terminal makes it easy to manage multiple Terminal sessions in a single window.

Navigating between tabs functions much the same as it does in Safari. To move between tabs, you can either click them with your mouse or use the Cmd+Shift+{ or Cmd+Shift+} key combination to move left or right, respectively.

I usually like to keep one tab open for the application I am developing at the time. I also have a tab open and connected to my Mac at the office when I am working at home so I can quickly reference something a few miles away without having to open up a new window.

Profiles

Terminal profiles let you save different settings for a Terminal window such as color, window size, and key mapping. You can customize the attributes of a Terminal window by going to the Terminal application's preferences window and selecting the Settings tab (see Figure 20-5).

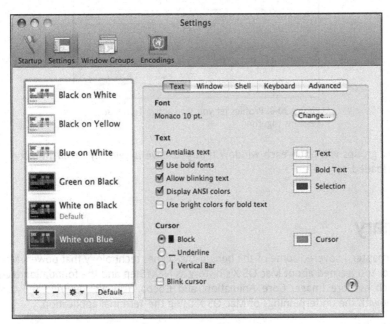

Figure 20-5. The Settings preferences area lets you define settings for your terminal session, such as the color and font used in your sessions.

A window profile lets you adjust several different parameters for your window. You can, for example, adjust the text color and font style, type of cursor, window background, and size. You can also perform more advanced operations such as running a command like ls at the beginning of each window session.

If you want to use one of the six profiles Apple includes or one of your own as your default profile for any new window, select it and click the Default button. From that point forward, any new window you open will inherit the attributes of the default profile.

Window groups

If you typically open three windows automatically, window groups can save you some keystrokes. Window groups remember profile settings, window positions, and tabs. To save a window group, go to the Window menu in Terminal and select Save Windows As Group. A window will pop up as shown in Figure 20-6 that will let you define what to call your group.

You also have the option of having a window group open whenever you open Terminal. This is useful if you have the same set of windows open each time you want to work with Terminal.

Figure 20-6. Profiles let you save active Terminal sessions together.

Window groups will open each window that you have previously saved with the correct profile loaded.

Summary

In this chapter, I covered some of the behind-the-scenes technology that powers Mac OS X Leopard. You learned about Mac OS X's history as NeXTStep and the foundation technologies such as Core Image, Core Animation, and Cocoa. You also learned the basics of working with the underpinnings of Mac OS X using the Terminal application.

In the next chapter, I'll give you a high-level look at the applications Apple ships to allow you to build Mac OS X scripts and applications on your own.

21 DEVELOPER TOOLS

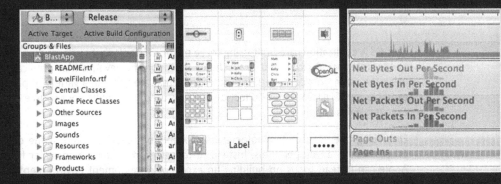

In this chapter, I will cover the following topics:

- Developing for the Mac
- Xcode
- Interface Builder
- Xray
- Dashcode
- AppleScript

After you have worked with your Mac for a while, it's possible there may come a time when you can't find a piece of software to suit your needs. Maybe you are in a specialized business or need a quick utility application or Dashboard widget to make your life a bit easier.

If you are technically inclined, you can choose to develop software. Apple has made it incredibly easy to get started with developing software in that it bundles its developer tools with every Mac it sells and every retail copy of Mac OS X. By lowering the barrier to entry for developing on the Mac platform, Apple has hoped to lure developers to the platform.

Think about it. It's no secret that Windows is the dominant operating system in the world. Because of this, most software developed is made for Windows. That doesn't necessarily mean that it's better to develop for Windows—only that you are reaching a larger audience. Microsoft's Visual Studio developer suite can cost up to thousands of dollars. That's a hefty investment.

By releasing its full suite of developer tools at no cost, Apple is inviting software developers from all platforms to test the Mac waters for free (other than the cost of hardware).

Microsoft has released "express" versions of Visual C# and Visual Basic for free, but they do lack some features developers may need. To get those, you still need to pay for the full version of the suite.

Mac OS X applications are built using three major IDE tools that I will cover in this chapter: Xcode, Interface Builder, and Xray. Under the hood, however, a Mac application is built using the same Unix compilers and other tools that are used on a variety of platforms. For example, the GNU Compiler Collection (GCC) is used to compile your source code into an executable Mac application.

Embracing open source technologies helps Apple by relieving some of the development process for its developer tools. Instead of focusing on building a compiler from scratch, Apple can instead focus on building an excellent development environment around the GCC compiler. Using free and open source software lowers the cost of development for the Mac OS X developer tools, which helps Apple offer its tools for free.

Cocoa

Mac applications can be built using two main development frameworks: Cocoa and Carbon. Cocoa is the preferred development environment for Mac OS X at this point and is centered around the Objective-C language. Objective-C is an extension to the C language that gives it more object-oriented properties and a new syntax. By default, C is a procedural language, which is a step-by-step way of writing software. In other words, a method calls another method, and so on, in a predefined order.

Object-oriented programming, on the other hand, is based on the primary notion that software is based on predefined objects that describe the behaviors and attributes of a person, place, thing, or idea. For example, if you were building an accounting application, you might have objects that describe accounts and transactions.

Besides being more object oriented, Objective-C embraces a square-bracketed syntax to code with. The bracketed syntax is a bit different from many other languages and may take some getting used to.

```
-(id) initAsDefaultOfType:(COItemType)type {
    return [self initWithTitle:[self defaultTitleForType:type]
        type:type];
}
```

21

Know how to program in Python or Ruby? With Mac OS X Leopard, Apple officially supports a bridge between those languages and the Cocoa framework. The barrier to entry is even lower for developing Mac applications!

If you are interested in learning more about developing Mac applications with Cocoa, check out Cocoa Dev Central at www.cocoadevcentral.com/.

Carbon

Carbon is the legacy framework that Apple developed to help software developers port their Mac OS 9 applications to Mac OS X. Carbon is based on native C rather than Objective-C. An example of a major Carbon application is Microsoft Office.

Carbon is still being used for development, so you can certainly choose it to develop a new Mac application, but the general consensus is that if you are developing an application from scratch, Cocoa is the framework to choose.

Xcode

No matter what language you choose to develop your Mac applications with, the preferred development environment for those applications is Apple's Xcode integrated development environment (IDE). Xcode, shown in Figure 21-1, supports development using Cocoa, Carbon, Objective-C++, Java, and AppleScript.

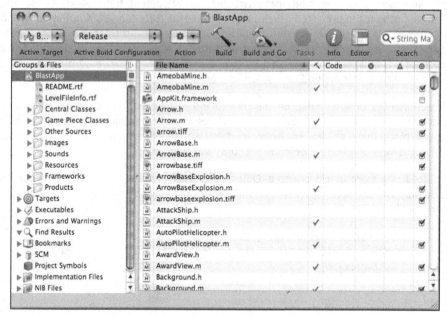

Figure 21-1. The Xcode IDE lets you build Mac applications easily.

Besides the standard compiling and debugging of source code, Xcode supports many unique and useful features that help developers build applications including the following:

- **Project snapshots**: Project snapshots serve as a sort of internal source control management system for Xcode. If you want to test out a new feature in your code, you can create a snapshot and work with it. If you decide the code won't work out, you can easily go back to a previous snapshot of your code without having to do any code cleanup.

- **Code folding**: Code folding is a feature that was made popular by the TextMate text editor for the Mac (http://macromates.com). Folding lets you hide the implementation details of a method or function until you want to view it. This makes your source code files a bit more readable and easier to navigate.

- **Data modeling**: Data modeling is a feature that was introduced in Mac OS X Tiger with the Core Data framework. Core Data makes it easy to build data-centric applications by defining a data model visually in Xcode and then writing code against that model.

- **Distributed builds**: If you are building a large application, it can be pretty resource intensive. If you are on a network that has several other Macs, you can harness their unused CPU power to help compile your application over the network using Apple's Bonjour technology. Distributing your builds across multiple machines makes compiling your code much quicker.

- **Research Assistant**: The Research Assistant is another new feature to Xcode in Mac OS X Leopard that gives you quick access to the API you are presently working with. Besides an API definition, the Research Assistant also gives access to related APIs and sample code that may be of use.

- **SCM integration**: Xcode supports CVS, Subversion, and Perforce repositories for storing and managing your Xcode development projects. You can check out code updates, commit your changes, and see the difference between your local copies and the repository copies.

Interface Builder

Without a user interface, an application isn't nearly as easy to use or useful. Apple's Interface Builder, shown in Figure 21-2, is a way to create user interfaces by dragging and dropping widgets onto a form and then interfacing with them via your Xcode source code. One of the major benefits of working with the Cocoa framework is that you can use Interface Builder to create nib files that store your interfaces rather than developing the interface manually in code.

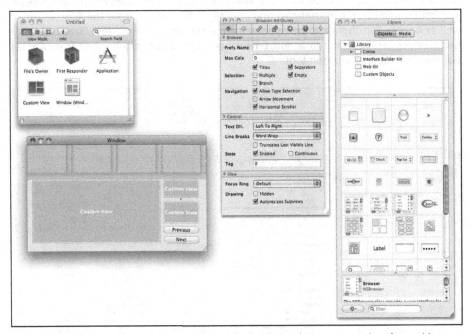

Figure 21-2. Using Interface Builder, you can rapidly develop and test your user interfaces with minimal effort.

With Mac OS X Leopard, Interface Builder has received a complete overhaul to give it a more modern interface and logical workflow. The previous version of the application was rooted in Mac OS X's NeXT ancestry. Interface Builder 3.0 also adds support for easily adding Core Animation effects to your interface with a few button clicks.

Besides building your interface, you can also visually connect buttons and other interface attributes to application controllers by dragging a connection between the interface item and the controller, all inside Interface Builder. Xcode is then able to understand these relationships and let you work with them in the code.

Xray

Xray is a new developer tool bundled with Mac OS X Leopard that lets you inspect the behind-the-scenes workings of an application as you are building and testing it to diagnose performance bottlenecks. Using Xray, you can automate some aspects of testing your application, which can lead to finding bugs earlier in the development process.

Like many aspects of Mac OS X's development environment, Xray is based on open source software. Apple integrated Sun's DTrace framework as the power behind the Xray interface. DTrace was the first open source release by Sun under its OpenSolaris project. Apple took the DTrace framework and extended it to work with their other performance tools.

Apple also put its own coat of polish on DTrace by putting a gorgeous interface on it, as you can see in Figure 21-3. The interface, while beautiful, is a complex and powerful beast. The left column lists the instruments that are presently running during the Xray session as well as options for displaying the options for the currently selected tool. Xray calls each performance test you can run an **instrument** because the interface borrows from Apple's GarageBand music production tool.

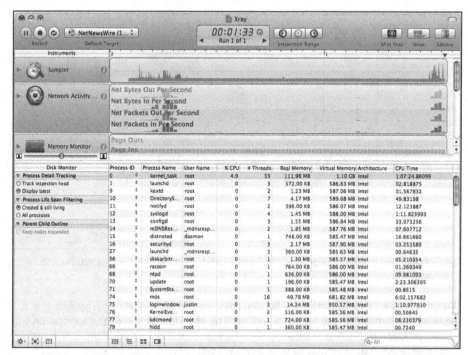

Figure 21-3. Apple's new Xray utility helps developers diagnose performance bottlenecks in their applications.

The right column gives you the results of the selected Xray tool. The top gives a graph of the output, and below it is a more detailed numeric view.

Besides testing CPU performance, Xray also includes tools for testing local and network disk activity, memory usage, and even the permissions of a file during its lifetime.

Dashcode

If developing a full-blown Mac application isn't your cup of tea, but you are interested in creating a smaller application, a widget might be for you. Widgets are built to solve simple problems in a quickly accessible interface: the Dashboard. Prior to Mac OS X Leopard, the process of building and managing a widget development process meant managing a complex folder of HTML, CSS, JavaScript, and configuration files.

There wasn't an IDE to develop widgets like a full Mac application, so Apple built Dashcode and bundled it with Leopard. Dashcode manages your widget development and allows you to debug your widget before releasing it in the public.

Dashcode's interface is by far the simplest of any of the major development tools (see Figure 21-4).

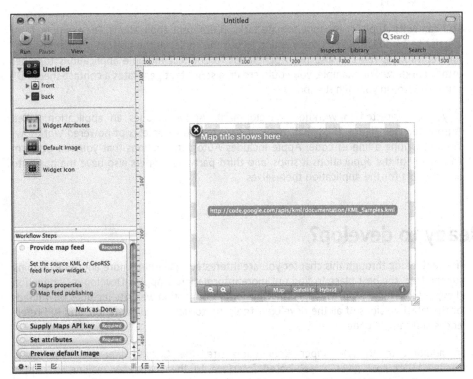

Figure 21-4. Dashcode helps you develop and debug widgets for the Mac OS X Dashboard.

Even though widgets are miniature web pages, tweaking the CSS can sometime be a tedious task to get your widget's layout perfect, so Dashcode lets you manipulate the interface by dragging and moving pieces around. Dashcode also eliminates the need to manually tweak plist files for setting configuration options for your widget. Instead, you can modify those values in the widget attributes view.

Dashcode includes several default templates for widgets such as a podcast or an RSS sub-scription widget, a countdown widget, and more. Besides using the default templates, you can also develop your own custom widgets.

AppleScript and Automator

If building full-fledge Mac OS X applications or Dashboard widgets isn't what you are look-ing to do, you can also automate some parts of the Mac experience using scripting. The AppleScript language was first released as part of System 7.1.1 back in 1993. AppleScript has a very English-like syntax, which is designed to make it more accessible to nonpro-grammers, as you can see in this example:

```
tell application "Microsoft Word"
  quit
end tell
```

You can write AppleScripts to automate tasks in different applications, For example, I use a script to modify Mail.app's reply action to put the cursor at the bottom of the message I am replying to. You can also use AppleScript to connect multiple applications together into a workflow. For example, you could create a script that generates a contact-sheet PDF out of photos in your iPhoto library.

If you're interested in workflow development, Apple includes an application called Automator (see Figure 21-5) that makes it easy to build AppleScript-powered workflows without writing a line of code. Apple includes Automator actions that you can perform with many of the applications it ships, and third-party developers also have the ability to add support for the application themselves.

Ready to develop?

If after looking through this chapter you are interested in learning more about developing for the Mac, the best place to find out more information is Apple's Developer Connection (http://developer.apple.com/). The Developer Connection web site includes downloads of the latest versions of all the developer tools, up-to-date documentation, and API refer-ences and sample code.

In addition to the Developer Connection site, the Cocoabuilder web site (www.cocoabuilder.com) gives a web-based interface to the cocoa-dev mailing list Apple provides.

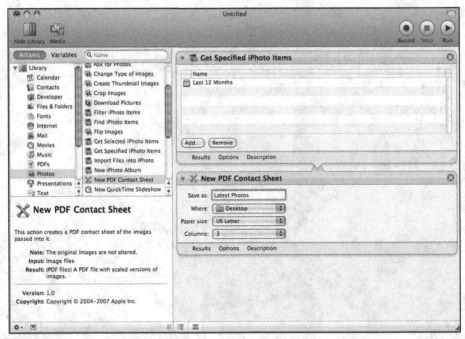

Figure 21-5. Automator makes AppleScript accessible to almost anyone.

Finally, there is a wiki for Cocoa developers that is another great support resource for Mac developers. The CocoaDev wiki, hosted by Panic software, is located at www.cocoadev. com/. The wiki hosts discussions about common problems Mac developers face and can usually provide a solution to those issues.

Summary

In this chapter, I covered the tools used for developing Mac OS X applications and scripts. You learned how software is built on the Mac OS X platform using the Cocoa framework and were introduced to the Xcode software editor and Interface Builder design tool. You also saw the new Xray performance testing tool Apple introduced in Mac OS X Leopard.

For those who don't want to create full Mac applications, I discussed Dashcode, which makes it easy to build Dashboard widgets. I also explained how to use AppleScript and Automator to script Mac OS X.

APPENDIX A SWITCHING FROM WINDOWS TO MAC OS X SOFTWARE

Part of switching to a new computing platform is learning the "ins and outs" of the new system and getting accustomed to making it work for you, not against you. A large part of the adjustment is finding the right application on this new platform to get the job done. Since you're considering switching to a Mac or have already done so, you'll no doubt want to use the documents and data from your previous computer—that is, unless a horrible Windows virus eradicated all of them.

Laugh as you might, but it's happened before, and no doubt could happen again. For some, losing their data to a Windows virus has been the final straw in convincing them to switch to a Mac.

Back in 2000 when OS X was still in beta, the number of applications available for OS X was still in the triple digits. Thanks in part to a huge independent developer base, the sheer number of applications for OS X has grown. At Apple's developer conference, WWDC, Steve Jobs announced that there are over 10,000 applications available for OS X. That's a lot of choice for consumers.

While you probably won't ever need that many applications on OS X, it's good to know that there are plenty of choices out there.

Why can't I just use my Windows apps?

One of the first things switchers come to realize is that they can't use their Windows software easily on the Mac. Sure, you can buy a copy of Parallels Desktop to accomplish the task, but what is the point to having a Mac if you are spending most of your time emulating Windows?

The Mac and the PC, while both personal computers, are different in one important aspect: they run different operating systems. The PC primarily uses Microsoft Windows, while the Mac uses Mac OS X. Each operating system takes its own approach to how it is implemented and how applications are developed. What does that mean? Well, think of buying a new Volkswagen Jetta TDI. The TDI uses a diesel engine. The diesel gives the car excellent gas mileage, pretty decent performance, and a little bit of extra cash in your pocket. What is the only problem? Finding diesel. You can look on any street corner and find a gas station selling unleaded gas, but finding one with a diesel pump or two can sometimes prove difficult if you live in the middle of Indiana like I do. You can't put a tank of unleaded or premium in your car and expect it to run, just like you can't open a Windows application on the Mac. They have different architectures powering them.

As for the Windows software you already paid for, there may be some hope. If you have a Windows license for an application and know it has a Macintosh counterpart, you can usually get in touch with the developer and get some sort of deal on switching your license to your new platform. Sometimes the company will charge a fee, but you may get lucky and not have to worry with that.

Knowing your workflow

The applications you normally use on a daily basis are probably totally different from those of, say, your next-door neighbor or the person possibly sitting in the cubicle next to you, or even mine. What matters is that you know your workflow, and this appendix will help you find the applications you'll need to find on OS X to get your work done. To help you realize what applications you'll need on your new Mac, make a list of the tasks you use your computer for.

Try and leave out the function of the software; instead, focus on tasks. For example, if you write your dear old grandmother often, think of that as *writing grandma an e-mail*. You don't need to say that you *open up Microsoft Outlook, click File ➤ New E-mail . . .* you just write an e-mail.

By listing the kinds of things you do on your computer, it's easier to understand the types of applications you'll need to accomplish those tasks instead of specific applications. If, say, you want to use SmartFTP and only SmartFTP as the FTP client on your new Mac, you're going to waste a lot of time looking for it—some software just isn't available for Macs. That doesn't mean there isn't some great FTP client out there that could take its place, just that you need to find one for OS X.

So to reiterate: what's important is knowing what tasks you use your computer for so that when you make the switch, you can find the types of applications you'll need, if no Mac OS X version exists for what you currently use.

A

The great hunt

So now you've got your list of tasks you use your computer for. All you have to do is go out and find the software for OS X that will allow you to accomplish your tasks—but where do you start?

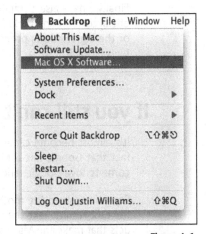

Well, the good folks at Apple have already thought of that. If you're new to OS X or even if you're not, take a look at the third option on the Apple menu (in the top-left corner of your screen): Mac OS X Software (see Figure A-1).

When you click this option, OS X will automatically open up your default web browser and take you to www.apple.com/downloads/macosx/.

What's this? Apple has taken the lead and put together a fairly nice directory of OS X–specific software, sorted by category. Notice what I said: "sorted by category." So if you're looking for a great tax software program, you'll know to look under the Business & Finance category.

Figure A-1.
The Mac OS X Software option in the Apple menu takes you to Apple's software download page.

What's especially useful about the category listing Apple has put together is that you don't need to know the name of the software you're looking for, only the type of software.

Remember that list of tasks you put together earlier? This is where it comes in handy. Looking for an application to draw symbols and flow charts, and take on the same relative features of Microsoft Visio? Then maybe OmniGraffle (www.omnigroup.com/omnigraffle/) is for you. Need to resize some digital pictures and export them out to the Web, but don't have the budget for Adobe Photoshop? Then you might want to try Graphic Converter (www.graphicconverter.net/).

More often than not in your hunt for that one app, you'll know what you're looking for, but you won't know what it's named. That's where Apple's directory will come in handy.

Other ways of finding software

If you can't find just the right application you're looking for on Apple's web site, there are many more places you can go to. Similar to the category directory, Apple has put together VersionTracker (www.versiontracker.com/) and MacUpdate (www.macupdate.com/) to present a more robust offering of Mac software. Both offer extensive search capabilities and probably the nicest feature: finding out what the latest version of a particular software program is.

Other great resources for finding software and applications specifically for your Mac are the I Use This web site (http://osx.iusethis.com/) and the Apple Product Guide (http://guide.apple.com/), the latter of which is often updated with offerings from various Mac software vendors.

Finally, I have also compiled a small list of Mac apps (Appendix B) that should prove beneficial to someone looking for that specific Windows application for the Mac. It lists many of the big Windows programs for certain categories and recommends a few Mac alternatives to each.

If you still can't find it

It's almost become cliché, but "when in doubt, Google it." A lot of people overlook the fact that Google has a Mac-specific search feature and many Apple Usenet groups. I've come to love Google, and so should you.

Sometimes even the most extensive and exhaustive search efforts on your part can yield the best results. Take the time to get to know your new platform, find the shareware products that make the Mac so great, and kiss Windows goodbye forever.

APPENDIX B **THE MAC APPS LIST**

Office suites

Microsoft Office: www.microsoft.com/mac/

NeoOffice: www.planamesa.com/neojava/en/index.php

Apple iWork: www.apple.com/iwork/

E-mail clients

Apple Mail: Bundled with Mac OS X

Microsoft Entourage: www.microsoft.com/mac/

MailSmith: www.barebones.com/products/mailsmith/

Thunderbird: www.mozilla.org/products/thunderbird/

CTM PowerMail: www.ctmdev.com/powermail5.html

Eudora: www.eudora.com/email/features/mac/

Web browsers

Safari: Bundled with Mac OS X

Firefox: www.mozilla.org/products/firefox/

Camino: www.caminobrowser.org

Opera: www.opera.com/

OmniWeb: www.omnigroup.com/applications/omniweb/

Instant messaging

iChat: Bundled with Mac OS X

Adium: www.adiumx.com

Yahoo! Messenger: http://messenger.yahoo.com/

MSN Messenger: www.microsoft.com/mac/

Proteus: www.proteusx.org/

Peer-to-peer/BitTorrent

Acquisition: www.acquisitionx.com/

Transmission: http://transmission.m0k.org/

Xtorrent: www.xtorrentp2p.com/

Azureus: http://azureus.sourceforge.net/

Burning CDs

Finder: Bundled with Mac OS X

Disk Utility: Bundled with Mac OS X

iTunes: Bundled with Mac OS X

Roxio Toast: www.roxio.com/enu/products/toast/titanium/overview.html

Disco: www.discoapp.com/

Organizing photos

iPhoto: www.apple.com/ilife/iphoto/

Aperture: www.apple.com/aperture/

iView MediaPro: www.iview-multimedia.com/mediapro/

Editing photos

Adobe Photoshop: www.adobe.com/products/photoshop/

Adobe Photoshop Elements: www.adobe.com/products/photoshopelmac/

iPhoto: www.apple.com/ilife/iphoto/

ImageWell: www.xtralean.com/IWOverview.html

GraphicConverter: www.lemkesoft.com/

Viewing PDFs

Preview: Bundled with Mac OS X

Adobe Acrobat: www.adobe.com/products/acrobat/

Adobe Reader: www.adobe.com/products/acrobat/

Making movies

iMovie: www.apple.com/ilife/imovie/

Final Cut Pro: www.apple.com/finalcutstudio/finalcutpro/

Final Cut Express: www.apple.com/finalcutexpress/

DVD Studio Pro: www.apple.com/finalcutstudio/dvdstudiopro/

iDVD: www.apple.com/ilife/idvd/

Watching movies

DVD Player: Bundled with Mac OS X

iTunes: Bundled with Mac OS X

QuickTime Player: Bundled with Mac OS X

VLC: www.videolan.org/

Flip4Mac: www.flip4mac.com/

RSS aggregators

Safari: Bundled with Mac OS X

NetNewsWire: www.ranchero.com/

Cyndicate: www.cynicalpeak.com/cyndicate/

NewsFire: www.newsfirerss.com/

NewsLife: http://thinkmac.co.uk/newslife/

Vienna: www.opencommunity.co.uk/vienna2.html

Building web sites

Dreamweaver: www.adobe.com/products/dreamweaver/

Sandvox: www.karelia.com/

iWeb: www.apple.com/ilife/iweb/

RapidWeaver: www.realmacsoftware.com/rapidweaver/

TextMate: www.macromates.com/

BBEdit: www.barebones.com/products/bbedit/

CSSEdit: http://macrabbit.com/cssedit/

FTP clients

Transmit: www.panic.com/transmit/

Fetch: http://fetchsoftworks.com/

Interarchy: www.interarchy.com/main/

Cyberduck: http://cyberduck.ch/

Scripting languages

AppleScript: www.apple.com/applescript/

RubyOSA: http://rubyosa.rubyforge.org

Telnet/SSH clients

Terminal: Bundled with Mac OS X

iTerm: http://iterm.sourceforge.net

Managing your PDA

The Missing Sync for Palm OS: www.markspace.com/missingsync_palmos.php

The Missing Sync for Windows Mobile: www.markspace.com/missingsync_windowsmobile.php

PocketMac: www.pocketmac.net

Virus scanning

VirusScan: www.mcafee.com/us/enterprise/products/anti_virus/file_servers_desktops/virex.html

ClamXav: www.clamxav.com/

B

INDEX

N

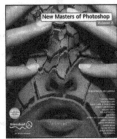

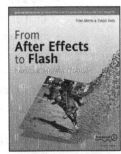

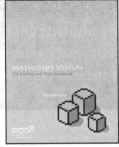

friendsofed.com/forums

Join the friends of ED forums to find out more about our books, discover useful technology tips and tricks, or get a helping hand on a challenging project. *Designer to Designer*™ is what it's all about—our community sharing ideas and inspiring each other. In the friends of ED forums, you'll find a wide range of topics to discuss, so look around, find a forum, and dive right in!

- **Books and Information**
  Chat about friends of ED books, gossip about the community, or even tell us some bad jokes!

- **Flash**
  Discuss design issues, ActionScript, dynamic content, and video and sound.

- **Web Design**
  From front-end frustrations to back-end blight, share your problems and your knowledge here.

- **Site Check**
  Show off your work or get new ideas.

- **Digital Imagery**
  Create eye candy with Photoshop, Fireworks, Illustrator, and FreeHand.

- **ArchivED**
  Browse through an archive of old questions and answers.

HOW TO PARTICIPATE

Go to the friends of ED forums at **www.friendsofed.com/forums**.

Visit **www.friendsofed.com** to get the latest on our books, find out what's going on in the community, and discover some of the slickest sites online today!

friendsof ED™
DESIGNER TO DESIGNER™
an Apress® company